Life of Fred®

Financial Choices

Life of Fred®
Financial Choices

Stanley F. Schmidt, Ph.D.

Polka Dot Publishing

ISBN: 978-1-937032-18-0

Printed and bound in the United States of America

Polka Dot Publishing   Reno, Nevada

To order copies of books in the Life of Fred series,

visit our website PolkaDotPublishing.com

Questions or comments? Email the author at lifeoffred@yahoo.com

Fifth printing

Life of Fred: Financial Choices was illustrated by the author with additional clip art furnished
under license from Nova Development Corporation, which holds the copyright to that art.

for Goodness' sake

or as J.S. Bach—who was
never noted for his plain
English—often expressed it:

Ad Majorem Dei Gloriam
(to the greater glory of God)

If you happen to spot an error that the author, the publisher, and the printer missed, please let us know with an email to: lifeoffred@yahoo.com

SPECIAL OFFER

As a reward, we'll email back to you a list of all the corrections that readers have reported.

A Note Before We Begin

Health is much more important than making a pile of money.

Having a loving and caring family life is more precious than mansions and yachts.

Am I clear?

Money can't relieve loneliness.

Wealth doesn't offer a meaning for life.

Agreed?

But having a decent amount of money can add a lot of pleasure in life. Being able to give things to your loved ones (and to yourself) is the ultimate reason to acquire wealth.

Having wealth can subtract a lot of pain.

Many parents don't teach their kids much math . . . or much about making a decent fortune.

I've written more than 30 math books (from arithmetic to several beyond calculus) to help fill in the "math gap." This book, *Life of Fred: Financial Choices*, will help fill in the "money gap."

This book might do more to increase the happiness of its readers than any of the math books (or the four high school language arts books) that I've written.

Wishing you great success,

Stan

Contents

Chapter One
Jane Austen

Fred turned to the first page of Jane Austen's *Pride and Prejudice* and read, "*It is a truth universally acknowledged that a single man in possession of a good fortune must be in want of a wife.*"

Small drops of sweat formed on his forehead.

When you are six years old, you don't want to hear that. He shut the book and put it back on the shelf. He stood there next to a wall of books in his office. Her words kept going through his mind. He went back to his desk and sat down. He sat on three telephone books so that he would be tall enough to see the top of his desk.

He needed some time to think. He thought Am I single? Yes. Everyone knows that. Am I a man? Almost. I'm six. Am I in possession of a good fortune? That's harder to say.

Fred took out a clipboard and did some calculations. He was much more comfortable doing math stuff than wife stuff.

He began with his income. As a professor at KITTENS University his current salary was $600 per month, which was more than most six-year-olds make. The salary schedule at KITTENS is unique among universities. They pay $100 for each year of your age. When Fred was four, he received $400 per month.

On the other side were his expenses. On the first Sunday of the month he gave $60 to his Sunday school. He was the only kid who paid by check. The money went for . . .

Different People Need Different Things

Be a friend | Help people who are in trouble | Teach | Dig a well to get clean water | Help kill mosquitos

Fred's clothing expenses were $6 per month. He hadn't grown an inch in the last couple of years. He seemed stuck at 36 inches and 37 pounds. When he went to thrift stores to shop for clothes, he loved to buy bow ties. He always wore a bow tie when he taught.

His housing costs were zero. He lived in his office on the third floor of the Math Building and didn't even have to pay for heat or electricity.

Food? There were nine vending machines in the hallway outside of his office—four on one side and five on the other. Occasionally, he would buy something and bring it back to his office. Then he would decide that he wasn't really that hungry and stick it in a desk drawer "for later."

The ants discovered where he kept his food. They loved Fred. His desk drawers never stayed full.

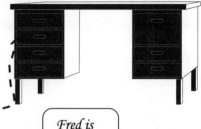

Fred is our hero!

$9/month for food.

The four walls of Fred's office were filled with books. He had never gone to class to learn the algebra, geometry, trig, and calculus, which he taught every day during the regular school year. On the average he spent $45 each month buying books. He found that reading was a much faster way to learn than heading off to a class and listening to someone present the material at a rate to match the average student in the class. And reading was much cheaper. Reading was also much faster than watching someone talk on television or on a web-based program.

He totaled up his expenses.

60	gift to help others
6	clothing
0	housing and utilities
9	food
45	books
total $120	

His gift and his books gave him the most pleasure.

Income $600/month. Expenses $120/month. Fred played with the numbers. $120 is what percent of $600? You divide the number closest to the "of" into the other number. $\dfrac{120}{600}$ which reduces to $\dfrac{1}{5}$ when you divide top and bottom by 120.

One-fifth expressed as a percent is 20%.
I spend 20% of my income.
I save 80% of my income.

Fred smiled at this thought. When your income is greater than your expenses, this is a very happy situation. In math, this is written as income > expenses.

small essay

When Income < Expenses

If your income is less than your expenses and your savings are all gone, then you need to borrow money and go into debt.

The biggest debtor in the world is the United States government. Year after year it has spent more than its income. In 2014, it owed more than seventeen trillion dollars ($17,000,000,000,000—that's 12 zeros) with less than 115 million (115,000,000) taxpayers.

Do the division. Each taxpayer would need to cough up more than $147,000 to pay for what has already been spent. Some taxpayers don't have an extra $147,000 to hand over to the government. (understatement)

end of small essay

Fred turned to his doll, Kingie, who was busy finishing up an oil painting and asked, "Kingie, do you think I possess a good fortune?"

Kingie had been given to Fred when Fred was four days old. (The whole story is told in *Life of Fred: Calculus*.) He was used to Fred asking him questions out of the blue. He wanted to ask Fred what motivated that question, but he was concentrating on his oil painting, so he simply asked, "Huh?"

Fred explained that Jane Austen said that if you are a man, if you are single, and if you have a good fortune, then you need a wife. He showed Kingie his calculations, which indicated that he was able to live on only 20% of his income.

When Kingie heard what Jane Austen said, he started to panic. He worried Do I have to get married? I am very happy here painting in Fred's office. But I'm single. But I have a large fortune.*

Kingie breathed a sigh of relief. He realized But I'm not a man. I'm a doll. Jane Austen's statement doesn't apply to me.

Neither six-year-old—boy or doll—was ready for marriage.

Kingie now had the job of explaining to Fred the difference between **income** and **assets**. He explained, "You have plenty of income. You are able to save 80% of what you make. Your income is the amount of money you make. But your assets (= your fortune) is how much you own. If you were making a million dollars a year, but had only been doing that for one day, you would have a high income, but you would not have built up a big fortune (= assets) yet."

Fred took notes.   Income ⇒ what I'm getting

Assets ⇒ what I have

Kingie continued and Fred listened. Kingie was the richest doll in Kansas and knew a lot about money. "The fact that your expenses are less than your income means that your assets will grow."

That made sense to Fred. He thought to himself If I'm making $600 and spending $599, I will be happy. If I'm making $600 and spending $601, I'm heading for trouble.

———————————————

* Readers of other Life of Fred books know about how successful Kingie has been selling his paintings. When Fred brought home a pet cat, Kingie built a little fort in the corner of the office to protect himself. He didn't want to become a cat toy.

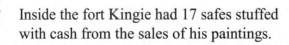

Inside the fort Kingie had 17 safes stuffed with cash from the sales of his paintings.

Fred drew a little chart.

Income	Expenses
Assets	?

There was something missing. He thought Expenses eat into income. **What eats into assets?**

Kingie took his paint brush and filled in Fred's chart.

Income	Expenses
Assets	**LIABILITIES**

Kingie showed Fred the painting he had just completed. It was the perfect example of asset and liability. Kingie explained, "Suppose I sold this car for $5,000. It is an asset worth $5,000. Now suppose I have a loan on this car for $4,000. That's a liability. The net worth of of the car is $1,000. After I sell the car, I'm going to receive $1,000."

Asset

Please take out a piece of paper and write your answer before you look at my answer on the next page. You will learn a lot more if you do that.

Your Turn to Play

Suppose you own an apartment house. It has income (e.g., rents). It has expenses (e.g., plumbing repairs). Its sales price is its asset value.

Draw this chart

Income	Expenses
Assets	Liabilities

and fill in examples in each of the four categories.

.......COMPLETE SOLUTION.......

My Apartment House

Income	Expenses
rents	plumbing repairs
	carpentry
	water, power, garbage
	property taxes
	interest paid on mortgage
	painting
	attorney costs for evictions
	insurance
	landscaping
	bookkeeping

Assets	Liabilities
sales price	mortgage(s)
	deposits received from tenants
	unpaid property taxes

Your answers might have been different than mine.

Chapter Two
Hiding Jane Austen

So Fred knew that computing his net income (his cash flow) by subtracting expenses from income ($600 − $120) would not tell him whether he had a "good fortune" (as Jane Austen called it).

His fortune (his net worth) would be found by taking his assets and subtracting his liabilities. Then he would know whether he needed a wife. (*"It is a truth universally acknowledged that a single man in possession of a good fortune must be in want of a wife."*)

Time Out!

There are two ways to figure out how well you are doing financially.

Way #1: Draw up a budget with income and expenses. Estimate your income. Take into account the time that you are unemployed. Then lay out how much you will spend in each category: food, clothing, shelter, entertainment, giving, medical costs, utilities, transportation, haircuts, hobbies, pets, federal taxes, state taxes, property taxes, Social Security taxes, and pizzas. (This last item is big for me, your author.)

Then each month see how much you have spent in each category.

This budget approach is often difficult. It's easy to forget to record the little items like the extra popcorn ($8) that you had at the movie theater. Money seems to leak out of your accounting. You can't figure out where it went. It's also hard to include in your budget those unexpected items: braces, bail bonds, and broken bones.

Way #2: Compute your net worth—assets minus liabilities.

Add up all the things you own.

Subtract all the things you owe.

Advantages of Way #1 (Budgeting)

❋ If you have a "spending problem" and can't control the urge to spend every dime in your pocket, then setting limits (only $20 for coffee this month) might help. Of course, if you have a spending problem, you might not stick to your budget when you are offered the new double-latte, triple-chocolate, raspberry foam, Carolina coffee with extra cream for only $7.

Disadvantages of Way #1 (Budgeting)

❋ You have to do it each month.

❋ Lots of attention to each of the items in the budget.

❋ Readjusting the amounts in each category if you spend too much in the previous month.

Advantages of Way #2 (Compute Net Worth)

❋ Fairly easy to compute once you have set up the asset and liabilities categories.

❋ Needs only be done once in a while—not every month.

❋ Much harder to deceive yourself. Every double-latte, triple-chocolate, raspberry foam, Carolina coffee with extra cream shows up automatically as less money in your checking account.

❋ It can be fun to watch your net worth cross the $100,000 and the one million dollar marks.

Fred computed his fortune (his net worth).

ASSETS

books	$500	(if sold—not the purchase price)
bow ties	$100	

checking account	$5200	
stocks	$	0
bonds	$	0
jewelry	$	0
gold, silver	$	0
pension	$	13
Total Assets	$5813	

LIABILITIES

credit card debit	$ 0
mortgage	$ 0
owe to Kingie for loan made last week	$170
Total Liabilities	$170

Net Worth = Assets minus Liabilities = $5813 – $170 = $5643.

That's a ton of dough for a six-year-old Fred thought to himself.

With celerity Fred hopped off his chair, went to his copy of *Pride and Prejudice,* and pulled it off the shelf. He thought **This has got to be donated to the library book sale. I can't have this in my office. It makes me too nervous.**

Just then, Fred had a visitor.

"Hi. I saw that your door was open, and I came to say hello."

Helen

Fred said, "Hi. You must be new here at KITTENS." Fred could say that because he knew the names of all the students at the university.

"Yes I am. My name is Helen. I have an office on the second floor. I'm the new English teacher. I know that it's summer, but I wanted to get a head start for teaching in the fall."

English teacher Fred thought. He tried to hide his *Pride and Prejudice* book behind his back. He failed.

"Is your daddy or your mommy here? I'd like to meet other faculty members. I'm from Troy, New Hampshire.* Moving to a new state can be very scary and lonely, but I hear that KITTENS University is a very friendly place."

The only word that Fred heard was *lonely*. She's single Fred thought. He dropped the book.

Helen picked it up. "You have *Pride and Prejudice*? It's such a wonderful book. The opening sentence is one of the most famous lines from English literature. *It is a truth universally acknowledged that a single man in possession of a good fortune must be in want of a wife.* That line has such irony. Oh. I guess I shouldn't use such difficult words like *irony*."

"That's okay," Fred said. "Irony is when the author's words are different than the author's real meaning." With alacrity he continued, "You mean that Jane Austen didn't mean it?"

"No. Some day when you are old enough to read, you'll find out that the only one who believed that first sentence of the novel was Mrs. Bennet who had five daughters for whom she wanted to find rich husbands."

Fred suddenly felt safe. He answered her first question, "My parents do not teach here. I do. This last June I finished my sixth year on the faculty. My name is Fred Gauss, but everyone calls me Fred."

You could tell that Fred was getting less nervous. Until he found out that Jane Austen was speaking ironically, the words *I do* would never have come out of his mouth.

"Oh, are you *the* famous Fred Gauss. I've heard about you and your teaching methods. KITTENS University is internationally known because of you. I'm sorry I made the comments about your mommy and daddy and 'when you are old enough to read.' When I first saw you, I thought you were a child."

---

* She needed to name the state because there are also places named Troy in Alabama, Idaho, Illinois, Indiana, Kansas, Maine, Michigan, Missouri, Montana, New York, North Carolina, Ohio, Oregon, Pennsylvania, South Carolina, Tennessee, Texas, Vermont, Virginia, and West Virginia.

Oh my Fred thought. She thinks I'm a very short adult. He looked at the computations on his desk and saw the words Net Worth = Assets minus Liabilities = $5813 − $170 = $5643. I hope she didn't see that.

She had.

"Who's the rich guy?" She asked. "I had to borrow money to make the train trip here. My net worth is negative."

Your Turn to Play

1. Many people in Fred's situation would lie. They would say, "Oh, it's just some fake numbers that I was going to use in a classroom lecture." Or they would say, "I was doing this computation for a friend of mine in Ohio."

There is a big difference between people who tell the truth most of the time and those who never lie. Fred doesn't lie.

If you were Fred, how might you respond to, "Who's the rich guy?"

2. Helen had $120 before she made the trip. She borrowed $600 from her sister, which she spent to make the trip to Kansas and rent an apartment near the KITTENS campus. She had an $18,000 student loan that she incurred while getting her master's degree in New Hampshire. Her earrings were given to her by her aunt. They are worth $400.

Compute Helen's fortune (net worth).

3. She found a studio apartment. She paid the landlord $200 in rent.

On the landlord's computer he has this chart:

Income	Expenses
Assets	Liabilities

Where should the $200 be entered on this chart?

·······COMPLETE SOLUTIONS·······

1. Always telling the truth does *not* mean that you have to say everything that is on your mind. If you are asked a question, you do not have to answer it (unless it's your mother who is asking).

✳ You are thinking of buying Stanthony's PieOne pizza restaurant from Stanthony. He asks you, "What's the most that you are willing to pay me?" You don't have to answer.

✳ You are doing 40 mph in a 25 mph school zone. The cop pulls you over and asks you, "How fast do you think you were going?" You don't have to answer. If you say that you were going 30 mph, that is called a confession—and can be used against you in court. If you say that you aren't sure, that can be used against you in court. If you say that you were in a hurry because you needed to get to a bathroom, in court the cop might testify that you admitted you were in a hurry.

✳ If she asks you whether this dress makes her look fat, you can comment on the color of the dress or ask what kind of fabric it's made of.

Fred could say that it's his assets, *but he doesn't have to*. He could ask, "Is $5,643 considered rich nowadays?" He could change the subject and ask about her train trip or whether she's found a place to stay.

Other people do not have a right to know about your personal affairs.*

2.

ASSETS			LIABILITIES	
cash	$120.	(the $600 was spent)	student loan	$18,000
earrings	$400		sister's loan	$600
	$520.			$18,600

Net worth = assets minus liabilities = $520 − $18,600 = −$18,080.
In accounting, −18,080 is sometimes written as <18,080> or (18,080).

3. The $200 rent is certainly income. But also notice that the landlord's assets have increased by $200. It is entered in two places.

---

* Of course, it is not a personal affair if it directly affects others. If you play your music loudly at 3 a.m., it is no longer just your personal affair.

Chapter Three
Her Office

Fred didn't want to answer her question ("Who is the rich guy?") and instead asked Helen how she liked it at KITTENS University so far. He figured that would be a safe topic.

"I just arrived yesterday. I spent the day looking at apartments and found a little studio apartment just four blocks from the campus. It wasn't hard to move in. I just had a couple of suitcases. Most of my stuff I left back in New Hampshire. I was living with my parents until I got my master's degree completed. This is my first teaching job. To tell you the truth, I'm a little bit frightened. I'm only 19 years old. On the application to teach here at KITTENS they didn't ask me about my age. I hope they don't fire me if they find out that I'm so young."

"I don't think they will," Fred assured her.

Before Fred could say that he was only six years old, she said, "You told me you've been here at KITTENS for six years. Would you be willing to help me learn about things here? It would be great."

Fred began, "Six years . . ."

"Yes, I know that six years is not an awfully long time to have been teaching, but my first day of teaching starts a month from now. A man with your teaching experience—I would really appreciate your help."

Fred didn't know what to say. He just nodded.

"Okay. May I first show you my office?"

Fred nodded again. He was hoping she would mention something about his being short. Then he could segue* to his being six years old. She didn't bring up the subject. She didn't know how sensitive he might be. Most men are not 36 inches tall. She didn't want to offend.

They headed out the door. Kingie started a new painting.

---

* SAY-gway To segue from one topic to another is to make an easy transition. Segue is also used in music: a transition from one musical section to another without a break. The *gway* is pronounced like "go away" shrunk down to a single syllable.

Segue comes from the Italian word *seguire*, which means to follow.

They headed down the hallway past the nine vending machines, down one flight of stairs, to her office. When they walked in, Fred saw a completely empty room.

"Oh no!" she exclaimed. "I still have your copy of *Pride and Prejudice*. I forgot to give it back to you."

"That's okay. You keep it. It will be the start of your new office library."

She placed it on the floor next to a wall.

"There is so much decorating I need to do," she said.

Fred explained that when he first came to KITTENS his office was also completely empty. He thought to himself **Decorating?** That was something that had never entered Fred's mind for his office. He just had a desk, a chair with three phone books on it, and his books.

Helen continued, "First, I need drapes for the window. Then a solid walnut desk with matching chair. An antique lamp. A wool carpet would be nice. The walls look so drab. I saw some special order velveteen wallpaper in the Super Elegant House magazine that would be perfect."

Fred's spending habits were not like Helen's. He didn't worry about the drab walls because he knew that over the years he would acquire books and bookcases which would cover the walls. He had asked the custodian, Sam, about furniture and Sam had taken him to the storage room where Fred picked out a desk and a chair. The office ceiling lights supplied enough light for Fred to read and Kingie to paint.

"Can you afford . . ." Fred began.

"A Ford?" Helen interrupted. "It is four blocks from my apartment to the campus. Maybe I do need a car. A new car would look a lot better than a used one. I wouldn't want anyone to think that I was some old stick-in-the-mud. What do you drive, Fred?"

"I've never owned a car, because . . ."

She interrupted again, "Oh. I didn't mean to get personal. I understand that you can't drive because of your . . . of your . . . of your lack of tallness." She didn't want to say the word *short*.

Fred was going to say that he had never owned a car because he had never really needed one. He could walk (or jog) to everywhere near KITTENS, and for longer distances he took the bus.

small essay

Spending

One important key to intelligent spending is sorting out your *needs* and your *wants*.

One morning when my younger daughter was about three years old, she walked into the kitchen and announced, "I need a pancake."

Her nine-year-old sister almost screamed, "You don't NEED a pancake. You WANT a pancake."

You need food. You like to eat out.

You need to get around town. You want a new car.

You need light to read. You want a fancy lamp.

You need to not sleep in the snow. You want ➡

end of small essay

"Oh, this is going to be so much fun!" Helen said. "I've got only a month till classes begin, and there is so much shopping to be done. This is the first time that I've ever been out on my own. I want everything to be special. I'm glad you mentioned getting a car."

What was on Helen's mind

How Fred Imagined Her Office

"And, of course, I'll need some fresh flowers. That will show my students that I care about loveliness.

"And several sofas so that we can sit and discuss Jane Austen and Shakespeare.

"A fireplace! I should have thought of that earlier. On the cold Kansas days, a cheery fire to warm us would be most welcome."

Fred's mind was racing. He had never heard anyone talk like this. He thought of *three different things* he wanted to say to her.

You don't need all this stuff	You don't have the money	The Teenager Paradox
A solid walnut desk and velveteen wallpaper might make you feel more special, but how special do you need to feel? Is your object to look good or to teach well?	Installing a fireplace in your office will cost more than the one or two hundred bucks that you have. Will you have to borrow money in order to eat?	Some teenagers believe two things that contradict each other. ① They are never going to die. Eighteen-year-olds will do risky things that older people would never consider doing. ② That they will never be living two years from now and having to suffer the consequences of bad choices they make now.

Before Fred could express any of these thoughts, Helen took his arm and said, "Come on. You know your way around this town. Show me where I can buy some furniture."

They walked down a flight of stairs and into the Kansas summer air.

Please write down your answers before you look at mine on the next page.

Your Turn to Play

1. When Helen had found her studio apartment, she had paid rent to the landlord. She also paid a $100 security deposit. This money is held by the landlord while Helen is renting the apartment and then is returned to her when she leaves.

The purpose of the security deposit is to make sure that she pays her rent and leaves the apartment in the same condition as it was when she moved in. If you ever rent an apartment, it might be a good idea on the first day you move in to make a list of every defect you can find and photograph it—every nail hole in the walls, every stain on the ceiling, every spot on the carpet. Then when you move out, the landlord can't claim that you caused the damage and withhold some of your security deposit.

On the landlord's computer he has this chart:

Income	Expenses
Assets	Liabilities

Where should the $100 security deposit be entered on this chart? This is not an easy question.

2. If Helen buys the cheapest hamburger at the grocery store, she is spending her money on a need. If she buys her lunch at *Harry's Hamburgers*, the purchase is partly *need* and partly *want*. If she spends $3,000 to get a fireplace installed in her office, that is satisfying her *wants*, not her *needs*. All of the KITTENS offices are already heated.

Your question: If Helen first sets aside $250 out of each paycheck she receives for savings or investment, is that spending for a *need* or a *want*?

·······COMPLETE SOLUTIONS·······

1. Assuming that Helen leaves her apartment in decent condition, the landlord will have to return that $100 security deposit to her.

So we know that he would have to enter that as a liability—something that he owes.

But the $100 has increased his assets while he holds that money. So he would also have to enter the $100 as an increase in his assets.

Income	Expenses
Assets	Liabilities
$100	$100

Since his new worth is Assets minus Liabilities, entering the $100 as both an asset and a liability means that his net worth did not change.

2. This is a hard question to answer. I could argue either way.

Argument for the $250 being a need: If a squirrel does not hide his nuts during the summertime (savings), then he might die during the winter.

If a person spends every dime of every paycheck, then when old age rolls around he/she will be in a world of hurt. First, all the "goodies" get sold: the wide-screen TV, the timeshare in Arizona, the boat. Then a yard sale to raise cash by selling the sewing machine, the lamps, extra clothes. Then. . . .

Argument for the $250 being a want: Who needs to save if you are going to work till the day you drop dead? Who needs to save if you will be happy to live on government welfare for food and shelter? Who needs to save if you plan to move in with your kids and mooch off of them in your old age. (Don't see Shakespeare's *King Lear*. It will scare you silly.)

Chapter Four
Furniture

Helen told Fred to take her to the same place that he goes when he's shopping for furniture. He told her that he couldn't ever think of the last time he went shopping for furniture.

"Does your wife do all the furniture shopping?" she asked.

"Wife?" Fred turned white as a sheet of paper.

"I'm sorry. I just assumed, since you have a son who does all those oil paintings."

"Son?" No one had ever thought that Kingie was Fred's son.

"I'm sorry. It was such a natural mistake. He has your eyes."

Helen thought for a moment and added, "But, of course, his nose, his neck, and his hair come from his mother."

She was delighted to learn that Fred wasn't married and that Kingie wasn't his son. This made him a potential boyfriend. She thought He is clean-cut, bright, and attractive. He's not married and has no kids. He's a professor at a university with years of experience. My office is on the second floor and his is on the third floor. I can see him every day and really get to know him. He is probably in his 20s, which is perfect for me. The only drawback is that he is so short.

Fred was busy trying to think of a way to convince Helen not to shop for expensive things. At the age of six, he had little experience with someone shopping for an MRS. degree. He suddenly realized where she could shop for furniture: at the thrift store where he usually bought his bow ties.

"I know just the place for us to shop," Fred announced. "It's only about two blocks from here. They have almost everything you need right there in one store."

While they walked, Fred launched into his you-don't-need-a-fancy-desk speech. She stopped. Fred stopped. There was one critical thing she needed to know before things went any further. She asked, "What do you do on Sunday mornings?"

Fred didn't understand why she asked that question. He said, "Sunday school."

She thought Perfect! He teaches Sunday school.

They resumed walking. Fred then started his you-don't-have-the-money speech and then concluded with teenager-paradox speech.

Helen's thoughts were elsewhere. This is such a wonderful time in my life. I've just gotten my master's degree. I've been hired to teach English at KITTENS. To teach English—that's the best subject at a university. To show my students that when they read great literature, it's not just for the entertainment of a good story, but to learn the truths and see the visions that the author offers. And then to meet this wonderful little man who is happy to spend time with me.

". . . and thus you see that with only one or two hundred dollars, the purchase of a solid walnut desk would not leave you any funds to live on."

"Oh, but Fred, there's no need to worry. I've got three wonderful credit cards that I received this last week—a Disaster Card, a Pisa card, and an American Depression card. I can charge up to $5,000 on each card and will only have to pay $80 each month on each one."

They walked inside the thrift store. Fred constrained himself from heading to the bow tie bin. He was here today to show Helen some affordable furniture. They walked to the back of the store where the desks and lamps were displayed.

"Oh, no, no, no," she said. "These are *used*. Let's get out of here."

Fred spotted a desk for $40 that was better than the one he had in his office. It was bigger, newer, and didn't have any ants on it. He thought to himself But my current desk is just fine. I don't need a bigger, newer one.

They left the store and headed down Main Street. Helen's eyes lit up when she saw . . .

As they walked in, they were greeted with, "Welcome *mademoiselle et monsieur.*"

Fred thought French? We're in the middle of Kansas. Helen, on the other hand, was delighted that there was such an elegant establishment.

Fred recognized the clerk. He was a geometry student that Fred had taught last semester. In a whisper, Fred said to him, "I didn't know you spoke French."

The student said, "I don't. My boss told me to say those French words to make the place sound more upscale. All I know is that those words mean mister and misses."

Fred whispered back, "Actually, they mean miss and mister."

Meanwhile, while the boys were whispering, Helen drifted through the store. (In a fine furniture store where they speak French, you do not *walk*, you *drift*. Your feet hardly touch the ground. It's much more elegant.)

Helen found her dream desk. The sign read, " *Solid walnut. Inlaid leather top. Massive, yet petite. Reportedly used by Louis* XIV. *The ultimate in charm.*"

Fred didn't know that a desk could have *charm.* He would have asked, "How much is this?"

She asked, "What are you asking for this *bureau*?"

The clerk was silent. Fred whispered, "Bureau means desk in French."

The clerk said, "Only $5,000." (He had been trained to say the word *only* in front of every price he quoted.)

Helen started to pull out her Disaster credit card.

Fred tugged on her sleeve and said, "Could we speak for a moment?"

Helen didn't expect a marriage proposal at this point in their "relationship," but she half expected Fred to offer to buy the desk for her.

Fred climbed up on top of the desk so that he could see her eye-to-eye. The clerk picked Fred up and slipped a piece of paper under his feet and set him down again. The clerk didn't want footprints on the desk.

"We need to do the math," Fred began. He realized that his speech about "You don't need this desk," the speech about "You don't have the money," and his explanation of the teenager paradox didn't persuade Helen. He had forgotten to mention that this $5,000 desk is *used*. The clerk would have pointed out that it's not used; it's an antique.

In any event Fred knew that math would convince her.

"If you buy this, put it on your credit card, and pay $80/month, it's going to take you 186.22 months to pay it off. That's longer than 15 years." (Fred was pretty good at doing math in his head.)

Helen thought Good. In 15 years my salary will have increased.

Fred continued, "That means that you will pay the Disaster credit card company more than $14,000 for this desk. (The math: $80 × 186.) If you say *non** to this unnecessary purchase, in fifteen years your checking account balance will be $14,000 larger."

Helen thought $14,000. $5,000 Numbers, numbers. Fifteen years from now is like forever from now. I like the desk.

She handed her Disaster card to the clerk.

The clerk giggled on the inside. He worked on commission (10%) and would get $500 on the sale.

The clerk went into the backroom to tell the owner of Truly Fine Furniture that he had sold the desk for full price. The owner, C.C. Coalback, was delighted. He had only paid $75 for the desk at the Nifty Thrifty thrift store.

---

* *Non* is French for "no."

Please write your answers down before you turn the page
and see my answers. You will learn a lot more if you do that.

Your Turn to Play

1. Coalback received $5,000 from the credit card company. On his computer he entered numbers in this chart reflecting his purchase and sale of the desk.

Income	Expenses
Assets	Liabilities

How did the chart change?

2. Helen bought a $5,000 desk and paid for it by charging it to her credit card. This is Helen's chart. Add two numbers to it.

Income	Expenses
Assets	Liabilities

3. Some assets retain their value for years. Other assets decrease in value quickly. In terms of retaining their values, how would you classify each of these assets?

A) A double-latte, triple-chocolate, raspberry foam, Carolina coffee with extra cream

B) A brand new snazzy luxurious car

C) A 100-ounce bar of silver.

D) A 3-day vacation to Yosemite.

Author in Yosemite
doing oil painting

·······COMPLETE SOLUTIONS·······

1. Coalback received an income of $5,000. He had two expenses: $75 to buy the desk and $500 commission to the clerk. His assets increased by $4,425 (5,000 – 75 – 500).

2. Helen's assets would increase by $5,000. Because she charged it, her liabilities would also increase by $5,000. (Actually, you could argue that her assets only increased by $350, because that is how much she could get for the desk if she tried to sell it.)

3. A) After you drink it, how much could you sell it for? Even if you don't touch it, after a half hour, it would probably have a resale value of 5¢. (The raspberry foam will be gone and the drink will be room temperature.)

B) The distressing thing about buying a new car is that as you drive it off the car lot, it is now a used car and its value drops by 30% in 20 seconds.

C) One-hundred ounce bars of silver can vary in price from day to day. One day they're $1,800. The next day they're $1,850. The next day $1,810. You can check the price of an ounce of silver in the newspaper every weekday. A part of the variation reflects the worth of the paper dollars issued by the government.

   The paper dollar is a fiat (FEE-yacht) currency—it's just paper. It is backed by nothing. Look at any of the bills. They say "Federal Reserve Note." In the old days (when I was a kid), they said, "Silver Certificates." You could go to the mint and trade the dollars in for silver. If you went to the mint today and handed them a $20 Federal Reserve Note, they might hand you two $10 Federal Reserve Notes. Paper for paper.

   The price of silver (and gold) has gone up over the years as the value of the fiat currency has declined. When I was a kid, my father bought me a banana split. It cost 50¢.

D) A vacation to Yosemite can be tension relieving. It can leave good memories (or bad memories if a Yosemite bear tears into your car to find food). But all of it fades over time. Ninety percent of the details are gone within a week.

Chapter Five
The Little Chapter of Horrors (Math)

F red had been told that the credit card purchase was $5,000. He was told that Helen would be paying on that loan at the rate of $80 per month. He knew that the credit card company charged 18% per year in interest.

From that he knew that it would take Helen 186.22 months to pay it off. Very few adults can do this bit of "mathemagic." If you don't believe me, read the first paragraph above to all the smart adults you know. Less than one out of a hundred adults can compute the 186.22 months.

❖❖❖ If you don't know how to work with percents, you are excused from reading the rest of this chapter. Please turn to Chapter 6 right now. ❖❖❖

COMPOUND INTEREST CAN BE
A GOOD FRIEND OR
A TERRIBLE BURDEN.

Compound interest is interest that gets recomputed each payment period. **Simple interest** is much easier.

If you lend me $100 at simple interest of 6% per year, then as long as I borrow your $100, I will owe you $6 in interest at the end of each year. (The math: $100 × 0.06 = $6.) In three years you will make $18.

On the other hand, if you lend me $100 at compound interest of 6% per year (and I don't pay any of the $100 back to you), then at the end of the first year I owe you $106. If I don't pay you anything, then I am, in effect, borrowing $106 of your money for a second year. The interest earned on the $106 is $6.36. (The math: $106 × 0.06 = $6.36.) At the end of the second year I owe you $112.36. (The math: $106 + $6 + $6.36.)

If I don't pay you anything, then during the third year I am borrowing $112.36 from you and will owe $6.74 in interest. (The math: $112.36 × 0.06 = $6.74.)

At the end of three years under compound interest I will owe you $119.10. (The math: $100 + $6 + $6.36 + $6.74 = $119.10)

I, your reader, must interject a thought at this point. Compound interest vs. simple interest means the difference between $119.10 and $118. That doesn't seem to be a big deal. Why all the fuss?

That's because it is a big deal.

If Helen can save $5,000 when she's 19, and she invests it at 6% compound interest, do you have any idea, how much that'll be worth in 46 years when she's 65 years old?

I, your reader, would guess that it would be worth ten or fifteen thousand dollars.

The big surprise is that it would be worth $72,952.

Moral: If you save money in an investment early in your life, it will grow large over the years.

In this way, compound interest can be a good friend. Save $5 a day (by not buying a double-latte, triple-chocolate, raspberry foam, Carolina coffee with extra cream) for three years (a thousand days) and you have saved up $5,000, which will turn into $72,952 in cold, hard cash when you retire, which is the time you'll need it most. This is not just numbers. This is real money.

➠ After 1 year, $5,000 becomes $5,300.   In math: $5,000 \times 1.06$
➠ After 2 years, $5,000 becomes $5,618. In math: $5,000 \times 1.06 \times 1.06$

✧✧✧ *If you haven't had beginning algebra, you are excused from reading the rest of this chapter. We are going to use exponents. Please turn to Chapter 6 right now.* ✧✧✧

➠ After 3 years, $5,000 becomes $5,955.   In math: $5,000 \times (1.06)^3$
➠ After 17 years, $5,000 becomes $13,464.   In math: $5,000 \times (1.06)^{17}$
➠ After 35 years, $5,000 becomes $38,430.   In math: $5,000 \times (1.06)^{35}$
➠ After 46 years, $5,000 becomes $72,952.   In math: $5,000 \times (1.06)^{46}$

Wait! Stop! I need to know how you computed $(1.06)^{46}$. **Did you multiply** $1.06 \times 1.06 \times$

$1.06 \times 1.06 \times 1.06 \times 1.06 \times 1.06 \times \ldots \times 1.06$ **forty-six times? That would be a real pain.**

No sweat if you have a scientific calculator (one that has sin, cos, log, and x! keys). They are cheap. Less than $20. And that's the last calculator you ever need to buy. It will take you through all of calculus. I have never owned one of those fancy graphing calculators, which cost about $100.

One of the keys on my scientific calculator is an exponent key. On mine it looks like: y^x. Yours might look a little different.

To compute $(1.06)^{46}$, I type in 1 . 0 6 y^x 4 6 and hit =. Out pops 14.590488. Hardly any work at all.

If Peter Minuit really did purchase Manhattan from Native Americans on May 24, 1626, and if they hadn't spent that money enjoying an extra large pizza but had invested it at 6%/year, then on May 24, 2013, they would have . . .

$$24 \times (1.06)^{387}$$
$$= 24 \times 6.214 \times 10^9$$
$$= \$148,140,000,000 \qquad \text{more than 148 billion dollars}$$

Compound interest can really work for you.

Or it can be a TERRIBLE BURDEN if you're paying interest rather than getting it. Getting compound interest is like having a fruit tree that gives you more and more fruit each year. Paying interest is like having a shark take a bite out of you each month.

Having a credit card or two is wonderful: ❶ You don't have to carry around as much cash. There's less chance you will be mugged. ❷ You buy something and don't have to pay for it for around 20 days. That's a free loan from the credit card company! ❸ Some credit card companies will help you get a refund or an exchange for a product that isn't what it was advertised to be.

But if you don't pay off the balance each month, the 18% compound interest will chew a hole in your future financial health. An unhappy old age awaits you.

Fact: Most people, if they continue to live, will experience the future.

Fact: You will experience one second of your life right now and years of your life in the future.

Fact: Three percent of Americans (3%) get to the age of 65 with any reasonable amount of financial security. The other 97% will *need* their little Social Security checks.*

I, your reader, am thinking of getting some high-income job—maybe law or medicine. I'm not going to be a part of those 97%.

Those high-income people do better.

How much better?

Five percent of them make it to 65 and won't need Social Security.

I don't believe it. Those guys are making more than $100,000 a year and and 95% of them can't even save nickels!

Yup.

So far we've done compound interest. You start with a present amount and let it grow at an interest rate of i for n periods of time. The formula:

$$(\text{present value})(1 + i)^n = \text{future value}$$

Example: I start with $275. I invest it at 8% per year and the interest is compounded quarterly (four times a year). How much will I have after 9 years?

✿ present value = 275

✿ n = 36   (9 years times four times a year)

✿ i = 2% (or 0.02)   (8% per year $\Rightarrow$ 2% per quarter)

The formula $(\text{present value})(1 + i)^n = \text{future value}$
becomes $(275)(1 + 0.02)^{36}$ $= (275)(2.039887) = \$560.97$

Since you claim to know beginning algebra (two pages ago, you were excused from the rest of this chapter if you didn't know beginning algebra), I can divide both sides of $(\text{present value})(1 + i)^n = \text{future value}$ by $(1 + i)^n$ and get . . .

---

* U. S. Department of Labor as reported in Denis Waitley's *Seeds of Greatness*, p. 115.

$$\text{present value} = \frac{\text{future value}}{(1 + i)^n}$$

This means that if I know I'm going to get $7,589 seven years from now and the interest rate is 5% per year compounded annually, then

* ✳ future value = $7,589
* ✳ i = 0.05
* ✳ n = 7

and the present value of that future reward is $= \dfrac{7589}{(1 + 0.05)^7}$ which works out to $5,393.36.

Money promised in the future is always worth less than money in the hand today.

Now comes the credit card (or mortgage) payments situation. Instead of paying off a lump sum several years from now, payments are made regularly (such as monthly) during the life of the loan.

The fancy word for a loan in which payments are made regularly during the life of the loan is **annuity**.

As before,
i = the interest rate charged for each period (such as interest/month).
n = the number of periods (such as a 360-month loan).

The formula for annuities (loans with periodic payments):

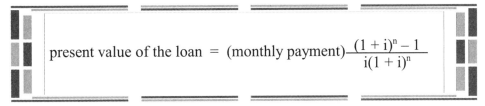

$$\text{present value of the loan} = (\text{monthly payment})\frac{(1 + i)^n - 1}{i(1 + i)^n}$$

You don't have to memorize this. All you have to do is stuff in numbers and get an answer.

Example: I make payment of $50/month and will pay for 60 months and the interest rate is 1% per month. What's the starting loan amount?

* ✳ monthly payment = $50
* ✳ n = 60

✻ i = 0.01 (or 1%)   (It's 12%/year.)
✻ I want to find present value.

Stick the numbers into
$$\text{present value of the loan} = (\text{monthly payment})\frac{(1+i)^n - 1}{i(1+i)^n}$$

and get: $\text{present value of the loan} = (50)\dfrac{(1.01)^{60} - 1}{(0.01)(1.01)^{60}}$

$$= (50)\frac{1.8166967 - 1}{(0.01)(1.8166967)}$$

$$= \$2{,}247.75$$

A more common question is, "What's my monthly payment gonna be?"
Example: I take out a $30,000 car loan at 6% interest for 3 years with
monthly payments.
      ✻ n = 36   (3 years × 12 months/year)
      ✻ i = 0.005 (0.5%   6% ÷ 12 = 0.5%)
      ✻ present value of the loan = $30,000.
Stick these numbers into the formula:

$$30{,}000 = (\text{monthly payment})\frac{(1.005)^{36} - 1}{(0.005)(1.005)^{36}}$$

$$30{,}000 = (\text{monthly payment})(32.8710)$$

and using beginning algebra, we divide both sides by 32.8710

$$\frac{30{,}000}{32.8710} = \text{monthly payment}$$
$$\$912.66 = \text{monthly payment}$$

Now you know how to compute monthly payments on an annuity. Simple
beginning algebra—just like $30 = x(5)$ gets turned into $\dfrac{30}{5} = x$.

**Hey. You forgot the problem at the beginning of this chapter—the
one you said that less than one percent of adults could solve. If it's just a
matter of stuffing in numbers into the annuity formula, most people can do
that.**

The problem at the beginning of the chapter told us:

✳ present value of Helen's loan = $5,000

✳ monthly payment = $80/month

✳ interest rate = 1.5% (0.015)

✳ we want to find the number of months, n, to pay off the loan.

If we stuff the numbers into

present value of the loan = (monthly payment)$\dfrac{(1 + i)^n - 1}{i(1 + i)^n}$

we get a mess: $5000 = (80)\dfrac{(1.015)^n - 1}{(0.015)(1.015)^n}$

The unknown is in the exponent. This is called an exponential equation. We routinely solved these in advanced algebra (also called algebra 2).

✧✧✧ If you haven't mastered advanced algebra, you are excused from reading the rest of this chapter. We are going to solve an exponential equation using logs. Please turn to Chapter 6 right now. ✧✧✧

There are very few readers left at this point.

Divide both sides by 80	$62.5 = \dfrac{(1.015)^n - 1}{(0.015)(1.015)^n}$
Multiply both sides by $(0.015)(1.105)^n$	$0.9375(1.105)^n = (1.015)^n - 1$
Transpose	$1 = (1.015)^n - 0.9375(1.105)^n$
Factor (a common factor)	$1 = (1.015)^n(1 - 0.9375)$
Arithmetic	$1 = (1.015)^n(0.0625)$
Divide both sides by 0.0625	$16 = (1.015)^n$

Two thoughts at this point:

1) All the work up to this point could have been done by anyone who has had beginning algebra.

2) It does take work to read these half dozen steps of algebra. If you did, you are rewarded by knowing your beginning algebra a little better.

So now we have an exponential equation $16 = (1.015)^n$

We solved these in advanced algebra.

Take the log of both sides $\log 16 = \log(1.015)^n$

Use the exponent rule (the birdie rule) $\log 16 = n \log(1.015)$

Since we want the number of months (n) that it will take to pay off this loan of Helen's, we are not looking for the exact answer down to the millionth digit.

Using a calculator, we find the logs $1.20412 = n(0.006466)$

Divide both sides by 0.006466 $186.22 \doteq n$
($\doteq$ means "equals after rounding)

And that is how Fred was able to tell Helen that her credit card purchase of $5,000 when paid at the rate of $80/month and at 18% interest would take a little longer than 186 months to completely pay off.

There are only two formulas for all this work with compounding interest.

The one for a single lump sum payment:
$$(\text{present value})(1 + i)^n = \text{future value}$$

The one for payments made regularly:
$$\text{present value of the loan} = (\text{monthly payment})\frac{(1 + i)^n - 1}{i(1 + i)^n}$$

Students often ask their math teachers, "When are we ever gonna use this algebra stuff in our daily lives?"

The material of this chapter might be one of the most common uses of algebra. Certainly, you will probably never use: If Jack can dig a ditch in 2 days and John can dig it in 3 days, how long will it take if they work together?

(Answer: 1.2 days)

44

Chapter Six
Human Nature

Helen bought the desk. It's that simple. Fred told her that she didn't *need* a solid walnut desk. He pointed out that she didn't have the money. He even used math to show her that she was mortgaging her future for a present pleasure. None of these three approaches convinced Helen. She bought the desk.

It made her feel good.

She was living in the now. The present moment is what counted. The future is a hazy shadow. It will never come.

If you have money in your pocket, you spend it. According to one recent survey, fewer than one American in four have the barest amount of savings, which is enough to cover six months of basic expenses. ☺☺☺☺ For three-fourths of Americans—those with less than six months of savings—are inches away from being dead broke. One event, such as a job loss or medical event, is all that it would take.

They get their paychecks on Friday and spend them on the weekend. They live paycheck-to-paycheck. It doesn't matter whether they have a high income or work for the minimum wage.

In psychology this is called **present orientation** vs. **future orientation**. This applies to all of life—not just to money.

Eat me . . . now!

Enjoying the dessert now vs. not being fat tomorrow.

Most Americans are overweight.

Staying up and partying all night competes with feeling well and pain free tomorrow.

The present pleasure of getting Daffy Duck tattooed on your arm and showing off to friends and years of embarrassment and long-sleeved shirts.

Sex now and years of regret.

Violence now because you were disrespected and years with scars and missing teeth.

We will have pain in life. That's a given. If you are future oriented, you will select the present, short, sharp pain (of not eating the tempting dessert, etc.).

If you are present oriented, you will grab the moment of pleasure now and have years of ache.

One last example: Learning stuff (studying) can be uncomfortable. You would rather be doing fun stuff. But without the learning, you have little to offer an employer. Have you ever seen old people working at fast food joints and having to ask, "Would you like fries with your order?"

Oops. I forgot to mention drugs, alcohol, and tobacco.

Double oops. I didn't mention getting a reasonable amount of exercise now. That will also make a big difference in middle age.

Now the opposing argument . . .

This is way too much. What kind of a life would it be to never enjoy myself? Never have dessert. Always go out jogging.

I'm sorry. I didn't make myself clear. To be future oriented does not mean "never-never-always." It's a matter of proportion. Fred splurges on bow ties. He has more bow ties than he will ever need. They give him pleasure. But, as we computed in the first chapter of this book, the kid saves 80% of his income. He doesn't need bow ties; he wants them. But buying them doesn't really affect his financial future.

Please continue with your opposing argument.

I really don't want to deny myself any current pleasure. I want all the fun stuff now. I don't want to practice the piano . . . or study . . . or exercise. I want to eat, smoke, drink whatever I want as I sit in front of the television or computer screen and vegetate.

One small thought and I'll let you get back to your argument. You can't have "*all* the fun stuff now." It's not available to you right now. Your choice is whether you can have *some* fun stuff now or a ton of fun stuff later.

But it's human nature to want to be part of the 99% who live in the now. As you wrote two pages ago, the great majority of Americans haven't squirreled away any decent amount of savings. I would feel like a real nut if all my friends are just joking around and I'm on a different path.

You are right. It is a part of human nature to want to go with the crowd. It's a big, broad, crowded freeway that most people are on. And many of them are not very happy.

The "different path" that you talk about is not well traveled. It involves . . .

SETTING GOALS
FOR YOUR LIFE

On that big, broad, crowded freeway of life that most people are on, they have no real idea of where they want to go.

They just get up in the morning and do their stuff. They watch television at night and go to bed.

They are dead already. Someone just forgot to bury them.

Here are at least five kinds of goals:

☑ Financial goals. The alternative is money worries.

☑ Physical goals. The alternative is how many older people look and feel.

☑ Family goals. Do you really want to have been married three times?

☑ Spiritual goals. Do you really not want to be connected with the Ultimate?

☑ Mental goals.* The alternative is to be uninformed about everything except baseball scores.

Ask the walking dead what their financial goals in their life are, and you might get an answer like, "Yeah. It'd be nice to be rich." But that's not a goal—that's a daydream.

A *real* goal is a target that is either hit or missed. Not "getting rich" but "having a net worth of a million dollars by the age of 40." Not "losing some weight" but "losing 30 pounds by July 1."

Your goals are your *personal* goals. Your goals will probably be different than others—if they have any goals at all. To have some definite aims in life takes real work. Most adults never make the effort.

☆ Write your goals down. On paper. Use a pen.

☆ Have long-term goals, medium-term goals (5–10 years), and short-term goals. Attach a date to each goal.

☆ Make your goals **so definite** that anyone looking at your goal and at your life can tell whether you made it or not.

☆ Aim high. These goals that you set are meant to pull you toward the life that you would like to live. Make them exciting, not boring.

These categories of goals—financial, physical, family, spiritual, and mental—are very flexible. One person's mental goal might be to be in college by the age of 18. Another's might be to write a play and have it produced in the next three years.

---

* As a trivial example, in terms of mental goals, I, your author, read 40–60 nonfiction books each year—on history, poetry, science, Christianity, economics, biographies, mathematics, philosophy. . . .

One person's family goals might be to have at least three kids, all of whom graduate from high school. Another's might be to behave himself in prison so that he might be reunited with his wife and kids as soon as possible. Another's might be to live a celibate life as a monk or nun. Everyone's goals are their own.

Whether you hit your target or miss it is secondary.

Whether you had a target in the first place is more important.

Your Turn to Play

1. What's wrong with each of these "goals"?

 A) I want to have a nice car.

 B) I want to take a walk for at least 20 minutes once each month.

 C) I never want to have another cigarette in my life.

2. Just before this *Your Turn to Play*, I wrote, "Whether you hit your target or miss it is secondary. Whether you had a target in the first place is more important."

 Let's debate that. You can take either side: agree or disagree with what I wrote.

 So that we can be more specific, consider a particular life. Let's suppose that his/her name is Dale.

 Suppose that Dale has been fascinated by volcanos since the age of 14. On Dale's Christmas and birthday lists are books about volcanos, movies about volcanos and a volcano T-shirt.

 Dale's goals include majoring in volcanology in college, visiting all the major volcanos by the age of 22, writing his/her first book about volcanos by the age of 25, and marrying someone who is also in love with volcanos.

 As a junior in college, he/she was writing a song ("Lava! Lava! Boom!") when a stray bullet from a gang war went through his window and killed him/her.

 Dale missed most of the targets. Now, on paper, argue your side of the debate.

.......COMPLETE SOLUTIONS.......

1. A) There is no date attached to this "goal." Secondly, what does it mean to have a *nice* car? This is not definite enough.

B) This goal has a date attached to it ("every month"). You can tell whether or not it has been achieved. But—really now—could taking one twenty minute walk per month be considered aiming high? For most people, this would be a forgettably insignificant goal.

C) There is nothing wrong with this goal. You can tell whether it has been achieved. For a smoker this can be a difficult ("aim high") goal to accomplish. It has a date attached. The goal is accomplished one day at a time.

2. Here's my argument for the pro side of the debate—for the side that agrees with *whether you hit your target or miss it is secondary. Whether you had a target in the first place is more important.*

It is, of course, sad that Dale had those aspirations and missed most of them. The world lost what might have been one of the best volcanologists of the twenty-first century. But Dale *lived* life. It was full of passion. Everyone who spoke with Dale learned how very special volcanos are.

Dale's roommate, Drew, majored in something else. Take your pick from art to zoology. Drew liked his field of study, but when Drew went out with friends, he never mentioned it. Drew got a job after college and died 60 years later never having made any real goals of life. Drew's tombstone had just his name and birth/death dates.

For years after Dale's death, Dale's friends placed lava-red roses on their volcanologist's grave.

Chapter Seven
The University Garden

F red was exhausted. Watching Helen spend money she didn't have for things she didn't need was really hard on him. He could picture her maxing out her other two credit cards* and spending years trying to climb out of debt. Many who fall into the quicksand of debt at 18% interest are never able to get out. They have money worries all of their lives.

Helen, in contrast, was elated. She had purchased a desk that might have been used by Louis XIV. As Helen and Fred left the Truly Fine Furniture store, the clerk moved the *Reportedly used by Louis* XIV sign to one of the other desks.

"Let's celebrate," Helen said. "What do you say we do lunch?"

Helen had read in a magazine that people who are au courant** speak of *doing* lunch. Most people at KITTENS would talk about *having* lunch. Fred, at the age of 6, thinks of it as *eating* lunch.

"I'm not quite hungry yet," Fred answered. "Let's . . ."

At this point Fred hesitated. Fred thought She is more than three times my age. She probably can't discuss math with me, but I could talk about literature with her.

I could mention the scene in **Robinson Crusoe** in which the hero is on the deserted island and finds the wreckage of a ship. He gathers up tools, food, knives and then finds a drawer full of gold coins. "I smiled to myself at the sight of this money: 'O drug!' said I, aloud. 'What art thou good for? . . . I have no manner of use for thee.'"

But I had better not. She might think I'm criticizing her purchase of that $5,000 desk.

----

* To max out a credit card is to charge a card up to its credit limit.

** (oh-koor-RON) Au courant = being up-to-date. In French it means "in the current." Au courant is not italicized because it is now part of the English language and not considered a foreign phrase.

I can't suggest our playing tennis. The racquets are too heavy for me.
Going jogging in the midday sun in the summertime in Kansas might not be a good
idea. Maybe we could go to the KITTENS library. She could look in the English
section and I could look in the math section.

Helen noticed his pausing and said, "Maybe we could go take a
walk somewhere together." She liked the idea of *together*. Heading to a
library and being in different parts of the book stacks would not have
occurred to her.

Fred said, "The KITTENS garden is very pretty this time of year."
He thought It's pretty, and not near any stores.

They headed back to campus, past the Math Building, the

university chapel, the tennis courts and
arrived at the garden. Fred had often
walked in this garden when he wanted
to just be in the sunshine. When you
live in an office with a doll who does oil
painting all the time, the smell of trees
and flowers is a welcome change.

"This sure is different than
where I came from, New Hampshire,"
she said. "But here in Kansas is where I
got my teaching job."

"Me too," Fred said. "Six years ago I came here because they
offered me a teaching position."

"Do you ever think of settling down somewhere else?" Helen
thought that she should have bit her tongue (an idiom) instead of
mentioning "settling down." Her mother had told her not to mention
marriage-related things in the first month of getting to know a boy. Helen
had known Fred less than three hours.

Her mother had told Helen that it makes a big difference where
you live. She told Helen that if you marry someone you no longer are the
only one deciding where you will live.

small essay

Deciding Where to Live

People live almost everywhere on this planet, but where you will be
happy to live depends on who you are. Knowing your own personal
preferences is the first step in choosing where to live. Some people love

living in San Francisco because of the many things to do there. Others can't stand the high cost of living in that city.

Some think that New York City is the only place to be because of the theatrical life there. Others couldn't take the triple layer of income taxes (city, state, and federal).

Some places are much easier to find work (where there is a shortage of good workers). Other places are much easier to find good employees to hire (where there is an abundance of good workers).

Financial considerations are certainly one important aspect of choosing where to live. I, your author, lived the first 46 years of my life in California, a state with high state income taxes. I moved to Nevada, which has no income tax. I knew no one in Nevada when I made that move. In the years I have been here I have made many friends and have been able to retain about two years' of income that would have been taken from me in California taxes.

Money isn't everything. Beside financial aspects of any particular location (cost of housing, availability of jobs, cost of food and utilities, and the tax burdens), there are six other factors which might be just as important:

CLIMATE

Do you care that there are 186 freezing days each year (Bismarck, North Dakota)?

Do thunderstorms bother you (93 days each year in Fort Myers, Florida)?

Can you live where it's both hot and humid?

Which of these really bother you: earthquakes, tornados, hurricanes, high altitude, or smog?

CRIME

Some places have ten times as many burglaries, rapes, car thefts, or muggings as other places.

In some areas it is a good idea to lock your car doors when you drive at night. In some places going for a stroll in the evening is less safe than sleeping with rattlesnakes in your bed.

YOUR NEIGHBORS

Are you comfortable living in a neighborhood where you are *different* than everyone else? *Different* can mean educational level, income level, race, religion (or lack thereof), or lack of appreciation of the local mania (whether it is the local football team, hunting, or dressing in overalls). *Different* can mean being covered with tattoos when everyone else can recite Leviticus 19:28 by heart. *Different* can mean speaking with an accent.

THE SCENERY

Some want the ocean nearby. (Forget living in Kansas.)
Others want the forests. (Forget living in Death Valley.)
Others love the desert. (Forget living in Maine.)
Others love skiing. (Forget Hawaii.)
Others don't care because they stay inside all the time.

THE CULTURE

Turn on the local radio. Is there anything you like?
Where are people on Saturday night and Sunday morning?
How are the public libraries? This is important to Fred.
Are there enough rodeo events for you?
Are the gun control laws too strict? There are places (as of this writing) where all handguns are prohibited. If you are a burglar, you love these places; there is little chance of your being shot when you break into someone's house in the middle of the night.
Museums? Ballet? Plays? Symphonies? Bowling alleys?

MISCELLANEOUS STUFF

Do you require special health care? If so, you don't want to be an hour's drive away from the nearest doctor or dentist.

Does your work ethic fit those of your neighbors? If you are a hard worker, you don't want to be around people whose main excitement is daytime television. If you are a bum, you don't want to be in a hard-working community where everyone is up at dawn. They won't appreciate your indolence.

Do you like it exciting and noisy (like some university towns) or do you prefer it quiet and rural?

Do you need to be near particular relatives, such as elderly parents?
Do you need to get away from particular people (such as the police)?
Do you do a lot of traveling and want to be near a major airport?

Most people don't give much thought to deciding where to live. They are rose bushes and stay where they're planted. They might miss making a move that will significantly improve their lives.

On the other hand, there are butterflies who can't stay in the same spot for more than a couple of years. They miss the chance to become a part of a community and have long-term friends that they regularly see.

I, your author, have made two major moves in my life: one to leave a high-crime area and one to leave a high-tax area. Both moves were well worth the effort.

end of small essay

Your Turn to Play

In order to help determine where are good places to live, you need to ask yourself a lot of questions about your choices regarding:
❦ Financial matters
❦ Climate preferences
❦ Tolerance of crime
❦ Ability to live with others who are not like you
❦ Favorite habitats
❦ What things you need in your neighborhood
❦ Health care/work ethic/noise levels/public transportation

As a warmup, mentally state which of these you prefer:
    A) A nearby forest or a nearby hospital?
    B) A good university or a college with a great football team?
    C) Neighbors who drop in on you unannounced or neighbors who never learn your name?

Now your turn to play. Create 14 questions like the above questions.

........**COMPLETE SOLUTIONS**.......

    Here are some questions I created. Yours will probably be different than mine. Answering questions like these and the ones you made up will probably make it easier for you to decide where you will live.

Which do you prefer (if you could only choose one alternative)?

1. A Costco or Sam's Club within 30 minutes of your house or lots of wildlife in the neighborhood (deer, birds, squirrels, etc.)?

2. Cheap electric and water bills or very little snow?

3. Living in a neighborhood with most people your age or being able to leave your front door unlocked at night?

4. Having convenient public transportation or being near a great pizza/ice cream/hamburger place?

5. A place that gets over 100° often during the summer or a place that gets below 20° often in the winter? (There are places that offer both!)

6. A place where you can go hiking without worrying about poison oak (which is the case in most of Nevada) or a place where you can go hiking where almost everything grows (which is the case in parts of California)?

7. A town where stores are closed on Sundays or a city where the grocery stores never close?

8. A rural area where your neighbors can own a junkyard (sight), a slaughter house (smell), or a rifle range (sound) without asking permission from you or a community with lots of CC&Rs (covenants, conditions, and restrictions) in an HOA (homeowner association) which prevents you from painting your house unless the color of the paint is approved by a committee?

9. A neighbor who plays drums from 7 to 9 every night or a neighbor who complains to you if you play your television too loudly? (I prefer the latter because I live very quietly.)

10. Living in a neighborhood in which you are a racial minority or living in a communist commune in which everything except clothes and toothbrushes are owned by the group as a whole?

11. Hot-air balloon races or plays by Shakespeare?

12. A place where most people are moderately overweight (most of America!) or where most people are thin and athletic?

13. A place where people offer an emendation of your first draft of an epistle to the governor or a place when people think that "an emendation of your first draft" has something to do with a commendation of a breeze? (There are advantages to living among people who are not smarter than chickens.)

14. A town where receiving government welfare is shameful or a town in which getting drunk is shameful?

15. Houses so close to each other that you can hear when your neighbor's toaster pops or houses so far apart that you almost need a passport to visit your closest neighbor?

16. People that talk about ① their travels, ② what they saw on television, ③ their recent operations, ④ sports, and ⑤ their pets or people that talk about ① world conditions, ② Austrian economics, ③ interesting (non-fiction) books they recently read, ④ the grim prognosis of universities in the Internet age, and ⑤ the role of artists and writers in a scientific world?

Chapter Eight
The End of the Affair*

Helen spotted a bench next to the pathway in the garden. She sat down and patted the spot next to her. Fred hopped up and sat beside her.

"Right now," Fred began, "I've been planning on staying at KITTENS. I've received many teaching offers over the last six years because my teaching [doing it the "Fred Way"**] has received international notoriety. Many of the offers are for much more than the $600 a month I receive from KITTENS, but I'm really very happy here. My income is much larger than my expenses, and my expenses cover everything I need or want."

There is only one thing that Helen heard in Fred's speech. It was "$600." KITTENS salary schedule for its teachers is unique. If you are 19, as Helen is, then you get $1900 each month. If you are 35, you get $3500 each month—$100 for each year of your age.

"Wait a minute," she said. "What's your salary before income taxes and other deductions?"

"My **gross income***** is $600 per month," Fred explained.

"But, but, but . . . that means that you are. . . ."

---

* Thank you, Graham Greene, for this chapter title.

** The Fred Way is Fred's unique style of teaching mathematics. He tells a story in which the characters encounter the need for a particular bit of mathematics, and only then does he present the techniques for doing that math.

In calculus, for example, he tells the story of a grocer named George and his wife, Cheryl. She sewed fluffy dresses for their two daughters, Fredrika and Meddie. (This happens in Chapter 10 of *Life of Fred: Calculus*)

Teaching the Fred Way, Fred avoids the question that almost every math teacher gets: *When are we ever gonna use this stuff?*

*** Gross income = income before deductions. **Net income** = income after deductions. Your net income is the amount that you actually receive.

Fred finished her sentence, ". . . six years old."

She picked him up and set him on her lap. "Young man," she said, "you have some explaining to do. I thought you were a short tall person. I mean a shorty—oh, you know what I mean." She was flummoxed by his admission.*

This was a new situation for Fred. Because he was only 36 inches tall, he had often been mistaken for a three-year-old. This was the first time that someone had thought he was an adult.

She asked, "But you've been teaching for six years?"

"I began teaching when I was nine months old."

"Then who is Kingie?"

"He's my doll."

"How did you learn all that math when you were so young?"

"I did a lot of reading while my mother was cooking in the kitchen."

"That's a lot of reading!"

"She did a lot of cooking."

Fred told the story of the dump truck that used to make weekly deliveries of cookie flour to their house. Buying flour by the ton was cheaper than getting it in 50-pound sacks. One time his mother stood too close to the back end of the truck and got buried up to her earrings in flour. It had taken Fred a little less than four hours to dig her out.

Fred wanted to change the subject. "I know that having a lot of money is not really your goal in life, but having money worries can make a dent in your happiness. Did your parents talk with you much about financial topics?"

"Not really. They were like most Americans. They made their money during the week and spent it on the weekends. I learned about checking accounts from one of my girl friends."

"What has surprised me," Fred said, "is the savings habits of fellow faculty members here at KITTENS. The history teacher who makes $3,200 each month, spends about $3,100 each month. The French teacher who makes $5,800 each month spends about $5,700 each month.

---

* Flummox = to confuse someone to the point of being unable to react.

It doesn't occur to the French teacher to spend $3,100 each month like the history teacher. In almost every case, everybody spends whatever they earn. It's almost as if they were ashamed to save."

If you got it, spend it.

Helen said, "Well, I guess that's not the case with me. I spend *more* than I earn." She smiled weakly.

Fred continued, "Baseball players and boxers who earn millions of dollars each year, too often are dead broke five years after their careers are over. If one boxer shows everyone his new gold necklace, then next week another boxer will have bought a heavier gold necklace. If one player buys a big mansion, another will buy a bigger one."

Fred wasn't used to doing this much lecturing on frugality, but he knew that if Helen didn't learn to make good financial decisions in the next decade of her life, she would probably be in a world of hurt for most of her life.

Kids grow up and rarely hear the first rule of finance:

Live far below your income.

This is not easy for most people. Most people, if they have money, spend it. Tomorrow doesn't exist.

So for most people, the only way to obey the first rule of finance is to pay your "future self" first. Each time you receive income (paycheck, allowance, gift from your aunt), set aside 20% or 30% of it. Put it *where you can't easily spend it.* Then live on the rest. And, of course, don't buy things on credit that you can't fully pay for when the monthly bill arrives.

Helen wanted to know where she could stash that 20% or 30% so that she couldn't easily spend it.

Fred said that it depended on two things: how old you are and how much will power you have.

If you're a kid and have a lot of will power, you can just stick that money for your "future self" in a special hiding place and never touch it. If you have only average will power and wouldn't be able to resist the temptation to raid the special hiding place in order to buy the rag-a-fluffy doll or the newest electronic thing you hold in your hand, then hand the money to someone you trust. Instruct them to only give you the money if there is a genuine need for it (rather than just something you really want).

If you are older, there are five places to stash those first dollars of each paycheck—five asset classes that will make even more money. When your money is busy making money, that's like having little workers slaving away for you even while you sleep. Get enough of those little guys doing their job and you won't have to work for a paycheck ever again.*

The Five Asset Classes
where money will make money

#1: Invest in **real estate**. There are many kinds: apartment houses, commercial properties, and, perhaps, your own home.

#2: Invest in your **education**. Books and online education probably offer the greatest value for your dollar. Most of the books that Fred reads are from the university library. On-the-job learning can be valuable, and it's free. And, for some, college.

#3: Invest in **paper**. These are the things you can't hold in your hand or touch: stocks, bonds, mortgages, REITS, certificates of deposit, etc.)

#4: Invest in **things** you can see and touch, such as gold or silver.

#5: Invest in the **business you own**. This is the big one. Forbes magazine asked 50 billionaires where they invested their money. Most of their money (77%) went into their own business. (Forbes, September 23, 2013, page 30.)

Note to readers: We'll spend a chapter discussing each of these five asset classes.

---

* I, your author, received my last paycheck in the month I turned 36.

1. Helen received a $1,900 paycheck. Deducted from that $1,900 was $300 for income taxes. In this chart

Income	Expenses
Assets	Liabilities

she would put $1,900 in the income box. Fill in two more numbers.

Chapter 5 (The Little Chapter of Horrors—Math) ended without any chance for you to practice. Let's remedy that. You may use your calculator on these questions.

2. I put $3,000 in a bank that compounds the interest once a year at 6%. How much will I have after 25 years?

The formula: (present value)$(1 + i)^n$ = future value

3. I put $3,000 in a bank that pays 6% per year and compounds the interest each month. How much will I have after 25 years?

The formula: (present value)$(1 + i)^n$ = future value

where n = 300 (The math: 12 × 25)

4. Ten years from now I want to have $40,000 in the bank so that I can pay for one year of college at Fancy University.

How much should I deposit today, if the bank pays 6% per year and compounds monthly?

The formula: present value $= \dfrac{\text{future value}}{(1 + i)^n}$

which was obtained from (present value)$(1 + i)^n$ = future value by algebra.

5. I get a loan of $34,000 to buy a new car. I will make equal monthly payments until it is paid off in 6 years. The annual interest rate is 6% and the interest is compounded monthly. What's my monthly payment?

The formula is

present value of the loan = (monthly payment)$\dfrac{(1 + i)^n - 1}{i(1 + i)^n}$

·······COMPLETE SOLUTIONS·······

1.

Income	Expenses
1,900	300
Assets	Liabilities
1,600	

2. present value = 3,000

i = 0.06 (which is 6%)

n = 25   (present value)$(1 + i)^n$ = future value

becomes $(3,000)(1.06)^{25}$

using a calculator   (3,000)(4.2918707)

                               $12,875.612

rounding $12,875.61 will be the future value

3. present value = 3,000

n = 300

i = 0.005   (The math: 6% ÷ 12 = ½% = 0.005)

                               (present value)$(1 + i)^n$ = future value

becomes $(3,000)(1.005)^{300}$

using a calculator   (3,000)(4.4649698)

                               $13,394.909

rounding $13,394.91

4. future value = 40,000

n = 120   (The math: 10 × 12)

i = 0.005   present value = $\dfrac{\text{future value}}{(1 + i)^n}$

becomes   present value = $\dfrac{40,000}{(1.005)^{120}}$

using a calculator and after rounding   present value = $21,985.31

5. present value of the loan = 34,000

n = 72 (The math: 6 × 12) and i = 0.005

        present value of the loan = (monthly payment)$\dfrac{(1 + i)^n - 1}{i(1 + i)^n}$

becomes   34,000 = (monthly payment)$\dfrac{(1.005)^{72} - 1}{(0.005)(1.005)^{72}}$

using a calculator   34,000 = (monthly payment)(60.339514)

algebra (divide both sides by 60.339514) $563.48 = monthly payment

Chapter Nine
Spending

Helen set Fred on the ground and stood up. She needed to walk for a while to give her time to digest all the things Fred had told her. In her mind, Fred had changed from being a possible F.M.* to being a F.M.**

"You say that I should put aside 20% to 30% of every paycheck for my 'future self,'" she began.

"Yup." (In Chapter 1 we learned that Fred saves 80% of his gross income.***)

"That leaves me with two questions. First, how am I supposed to live on 70% to 80% of my gross income, and, second, what should I know about those Five Asset Classes [education, business you own, real estate, paper, and things you can touch] into which I'm supposed to stash 20% to 30% of my gross income?"

"Those are called the Spending & Saving questions," Fred said. "For you, the place to start would be with your spending habits."

> *I have enough money to last me the rest of my life, unless I buy something.*
> —Jackie Mason

silly quote

Food

Buying at the wholesale outlets (such as Costco or Sam's Club) can save about a third of what your local grocery store charges. The temptation at those stores are all the other goodies—six-foot-wide televisions, furniture, barbeques, and three-hundred-dollar blenders.

Eat at home. Eggs offer much cheaper protein than steaks.

---

* Future Mate

** Financial Mentor

*** Fred is still young. I, your author, live on less than 15% of my gross income. I save some and give big chunks to my two favorite charities.

Time Out!

I'm not saying you should never have steak or never eat out.

It's a matter of paying attention. It's a matter of being able to live on 75% of your income. Depending on your circumstances, it might be possible to buy $5 cups of coffee every day of the week OR it might be the case that buying one $5 cup of coffee might be really stupid.

One major goal of this book is that you don't find yourself at the age of 60 on food stamps. (Currently, about one American in six requires others to help them buy food.)

Clothing, furniture, and cars

Do you buy clothing to make you feel good? Helen bought that $5,000 desk to make her look good. How much jewelry and how many shoes do you *need*?

Do you lease that fancy car so that others will think you are something special? Are you in the habit of buying a brand new car every three years?

There are people who will judge you by the new clothes you wear, by the diamonds on your watch, by the decor of your place, and by the kind of car that you drive. Here's the news: Those people don't matter! They are shallow.

And no one is going to judge you on the basis of the thousands of dollars you have stashed away for your future. Why? Because you are not going to tell them! You do not want to be judged by anything except the content of your character—whether you are trustworthy, loyal, helpful, friendly, courteous, kind, obedient, cheerful, thrifty, brave, clean, and reverent.[*]

---

[*] I memorized that list from a group I belonged to years ago. I didn't have to look them up to write them in this book.

Shelter

Do you need a place big enough to invite your four hundred closest friends over for a party? Does your place need to be cool enough that all your friends envy you?

One of the real questions you face is whether to rent or to buy. There are good arguments for each.

RENT	BUY
If you don't have the down payment or if you have a bad credit record, buying might be almost impossible. When your lease is up, you can move without spending five months trying to find a buyer.	There are transaction costs associated with buying or selling a house, such as real estate commissions, title insurance, and transfer taxes. If you are only going to stay for a year or two, it might be cheaper to rent.
Usually, the landlord takes care of the repairs and upkeep. Of course, this is reflected in how high your rent is.	If you own it, you get to decide which repairs to make and what color to paint your bedrooms.
Your rent can go up every time you renew your lease.	Your mortgage payment is fixed for the 15 or 30 years of the mortgage. Your property taxes can go up.
You buy renter's insurance to cover the things in your apartment. Your landlord buys insurance for the building, and this is reflected in how high your rent is.	You buy insurance for the house. If your house is bombed during a war, you lose everything (since insurance doesn't usually cover war).

Home Sweet Home Mansion

Haircuts, holidays, and C_2H_5OH

All the little things can add up. It's really not difficult to cut your kids' hair at home.

Fancy fingernails—announce that either you have money to burn or you are burning through your money.

Is a trip to Patagonia* really being frugal? How about a vacation in a local state park instead?

For too many people, drinking ethanol (C_2H_5OH) can significantly affect their ability to save money. First, because of its cost, and second, because of its ability to make you stupid. Did they mention in Sunday school about the time when Noah got drunk and naked? (Genesis 9:20)

Ever notice what a pack of cigarettes cost?

Did you ever receive gifts that were a real waste of money? The same might be true of gifts that you give. Are you in family or business situations where gifts are mandatory? It's been said that gifts that are expected are not given—they are paid.

THE OPPOSING ARGUMENT

Money is saved for only one reason: to be spent. It is just a medium of exchange. You trade your money for stuff that pleases you, such as new underwear or a pizza.

The miser who squirrels away zillions of dollars and skips going to the dentist is nuts.

You should be free to spend your money (and max out your credit cards) on anything and everything you want.

I, your author, agree. You are free to spend as you wish (assuming you are an adult and not in prison). The only question is whether spending more than 75% of your income now is *really* going to make your life happier. Most people spend it now. I am in the minority.

---

* Patagonia—some people don't know where that is.

Your Turn to Play

1. Everyone I know is in the minority in some way or another. Name six ways in which you are not in the majority. I'll list six ways that apply to me in the answers.

2. There is **one easy way** to tell how much you should indulge yourself.

Whether you buy that $5,000 desk or one at the thrift shop.

Whether you buy a $300 blender or the $39 model.

Whether you eat out every day or cook at home.

Whether you eat steak (or eggs or beans/rice, which also offer what is known as "complete protein").

Whether you buy the newest fashion clothing or wear what you already have. (I wear a tie every Sunday. Most of them are more than 30 years old.)

Whether you get a pedicure every month or just keep your feet washed.

Whether you buy popcorn at the movies or save $5.

Whether you give expensive gifts or spend time making something special for each recipient.

Whether you buy the newest pad/tablet/phone or use last year's.

Whether you live in a mansion or a studio apartment.

Whether you go on cruise ship vacations every three months or go walking in the local park.

That **one easy way** to tell how much you should indulge yourself was outlined in this chapter. In one sentence, state that one easy way. *If you can't, please don't just turn the page and read the answer. Instead, reread the four pages of this chapter.*

. . . . COMPLETE SOLUTIONS . . . .

1. Ways I am in a minority.
(1) I was a single father for years. That is not that common.
(2) I'm taller than most people.
(3) I read more than most.
(4) I am a tenor. Probably less than 20% of the population would call themselves tenors.
(5) I have never once tried cigarettes.
(6) I have green eyes.

2. The **easy way** to determine which indulgences are appropriate for you is easy to state but often difficult to follow.

> *I can resist everything except temptation.*
> —Oscar Wilde

silly quote

Your expenses (including credit card purchases) should not exceed 75% of your income. It isn't that complicated.

NEVER HAVING TO WORK FOR A PAYCHECK AGAIN

Sound good? How about retiring in **24 years**? If you are 20 now, you retire at 44 and live at the same income level *forever*.

The math: You stash 25% of your income in the Five Asset Classes (real estate, education, paper, things you can touch, and a business that you own) and make, say, 6% per year as those assets increase.

If your monthly gross income is $4 (to make things simple) and you live on $3 and invest $1 each month, then by the Rule of 72 (explained in the next chapter), that $1 will become $2 in 12 years and $4 in 24 years.

Each buck you invest becomes $4 in 24 years, You harvest $3 of them and the fourth is replanted and will be ripe again in 24 years.

The $1 planted on January 1 becomes $4 on January 1, 24 years later. The $1 planted on February 1 becomes $4 on February 1, 24 years later. The faucet never turns off. When you die and pass this along to your kid, he/she will have that income for life. Your 24 years of investing will last for centuries. All it takes is discipline *now*.

Chapter Ten
Retire in 24 Years

The cards, letters, emails, telegrams, and phone calls have been coming in by the ton* regarding that half page at the end of the previous chapter.

One email read:

Dear Stan,

All that stuff you wrote about

Income	Expenses
Assets	Liabilities

was nice, but RETIRING IN 24 YEARS is the best news I've heard in years. You gotta spend a chapter spelling that out in super detail—not just a half page. I don't care—you can even use math (if you have to), but this stuff really matters to me. Go slow. Talk lots. I'll pay super attention. This alone is worth the price of the book.

Love,

Mom

Okay. Here goes. I was going to spend Chapters 10–14 talking about each of the Five Asset Classes (real estate, education, paper, things you can touch, and a business that you own), but in response to your requests and in obedience to the Fifth Commandment, this Chapter 10 is yours.

---

* How many emails would it take to weigh a ton?

First, the Rule of 72.   If you tell me that you have some money that is growing at the rate of 6% per year (compounded annually), I know that it will double in 12 years.

If the interest rate is 8%, it will double in 9 years.

If the interest rate is 12%, it will double in 6 years.

The Rule of 72: Divide 72 by the interest rate and that will give you the approximate number of years for your money to double.

For example, if the interest rate is 10%, then in $\frac{72}{10}$ years, your money will double. That's 7.2 years (and I did that without a calculator.)

So at 6%, your money doubles in 12 years and doubles again in the next 12 years. It quadruples in 24 years. (The math: 24 = 12 + 12)

> *It is pretty to see what money will do.*
> —Samuel Pepys
> as he wrote in his diary on March 21, 1667

not silly at all

The Five Asset Classes are real estate, education, paper, things you can touch, and a business that you own. Imagine putting a dollar into one of those investments. Compounding at 6% per year, it would double to $2 in 12 years and double again to $4 in 24 years.

That might be like planting a tree and watching it quadruple in size in 24 years.

If you are more into cooking than forestry, you might think of a lump of yeasty dough that is set aside in a warm place to swell up.

I know. I know. This is not a lump of dough. Slices of pepperoni won't grow, but, please, let's pretend.

If you are a gardener, you might think of investing in one of the Five Asset Classes as planting a tulip and watching it turn into four tulips over the space of 24 years.

Now how does that allow you to retire in 24 years? One pleasant way to think about that might be called . . .

PLANTING IN A CIRCLE

Each month you "plant" your dough.

In the first month

In the fifth month

In 24 years you will have planted a full circle and will have come back to the first dough you "planted."

#1: You will never have to plant (i.e. save) any more dough.

#2: You can sit down and eat three-fourths of that pizza that you planted 24 years ago.

#3: In the next month, you can move on to the next pizza and eat three-fourths of it.

#4: Till the day you die. Then you have your favorite, say, granddaughter sit in your place and eat without working for all of her life. Or you can split this pizza garden into, say, four parts. Then each recipient will have to work less than 15 years in order to have a fully planted retirement garden. If they begin at age 20, each of the four will be retired by age 35. Your four kids will **LoVe** you.

Here's how to picture **PLANTING IN A CIRCLE**:

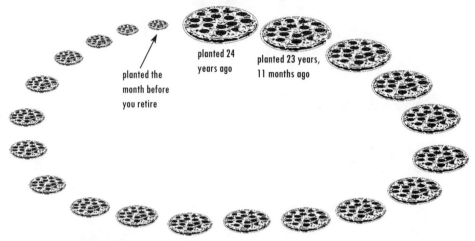

planted 24 years ago

planted 23 years, 11 months ago

planted the month before you retire

You have two choices . . .

 Doing it the Fred way: Save 25% of your income and grow it at 6%. Begin when you are 20 and retire at 44. The money you have to spend will stay constant (75% of gross income) forever.

 Doing it like almost everybody else: Spend your income. Begin at 20 and work till 65. Watch your income suddenly drop as you try to live on Social Security and a company pension.

It's that simple. Take your choice.

◊   ◊   ◊

Some happy variations on the Fred way:

A) Plant 25% of your income for 27 years, 8 months, and your income will jump to 100% of what was your gross income upon retirement.

B) Plant 25% of your income for 38 years and retire on TWICE your income forever.

Unless you have had advanced algebra (also known as second-year high school algebra), please skip over this box and go on to Chapter 11.

Here is the calculation to show you can retire in 24 years.

My income is, say, 4/year and I save 1/year and plant it. My net income that I live on is 3/year. (We're working in years instead of months to make the arithmetic easier. If we compounded monthly, the return for you would be even greater.)

Present value of the planting is 1.

I want to find out how long it will take for that 1 to grow into 4 so that I can harvest 3/year to live on. It grows at 6%/year.

The easier compound interest formula from Chapter 5:

$$\text{future value} = (\text{present value})(1 + i)^n$$

becomes
$$4 = 1(1.06)^n$$
$$4 = (1.06)^n$$

This is an exponential equation (the unknown is in the exponent).

Take the log of both sides $\qquad\qquad \log 4 = \log(1.06)^n$

The exponent rule (the Birdie rule) $\qquad \log 4 = n \log(1.06)$

Use a calculator to approximate the logs $\quad 0.60206 = n(0.0253)$

Algebra $\qquad\qquad\qquad\qquad\qquad\qquad 23.8 = n$

Which is even less than 24 years.

Your Turn to Play

1. In the happy *Variation A* on the previous page, you were told that working for 27 years, 8 months would allow to you retire at full 100% income.

There is no need to take that on faith. Repeat what's in the box above. Your annual income is still 4/year. Your saving is still 1/year. The only difference is that you want your planting to grow to 5 instead of 4. Then you will harvest 4/year to live on. Make those changes and compute n.

2. A harder problem would be to show the "work less than 15 years" (on the top of the previous page) if you are one of the four kids who inherits one-fourth of the completed pizza circle that your parents created in their lifetimes.

You want each pizza to grow into 4 pizzas. You are planting 1¾ pizzas each year (1 from your savings and ¾ from your one-quarter share of your inheritance). (Your parent's pizza circle generates 3/year and you get one-fourth of that.)

.... COMPLETE SOLUTIONS ....

1. Income is 4/year. You save 1/year. You want the 1 to grow into 5.

$$\text{future value} = (\text{present value})(1 + i)^n$$

becomes $\qquad\qquad\qquad 5 = 1(1.06)^n$

$$5 = (1.06)^n$$

Take the log of both sides $\qquad \log 5 = \log(1.06)^n$

Birdie rule $\qquad\qquad\qquad \log 5 = n \log 1.06$

Approximate the logs $\qquad 0.69897 = n(0.0253)$

Algebra $\qquad\qquad\qquad\qquad 27.6 = n$

27.6 years < 27 years, 8 months

2. Income is 4/year. You save 1/year. Your inheritance adds another ¾/year to your savings. You want the savings to grow to 4.

$$\text{future value} = (\text{present value})(1 + i)^n$$

becomes $\qquad\qquad\qquad 4 = 1¾(1.06)^n$

Divide both sides by 1.75 $\qquad 2.2857 = (1.06)^n$

Take the log of both sides $\qquad \log 2.2857 = \log (1.06)^n$

Birdie rule $\qquad\qquad\qquad \log 2.2857 = n \log 1.06$

Approximate the logs $\qquad 0.359 = n(0.0253)$

Algebra $\qquad\qquad\qquad\qquad 14.1 = n$

which is much less than 15 years.

These computations all look alike. By now, I hope that they are almost boring. (That's a sign of mastery of the material.)

Now you should be able to do any variation on this theme. You could compute how long to retirement if your Five Assets were yielding 7% interest instead of 6%, but you were only saving 20% of your income (shame!) Income is 5/year and you save 1/year. (That's 20% saving.) Want the 1 to grow to 5. Then you could harvest 4/year. $5 = 1(1.07)^n$ ... $n = 23.8$ years

Chapter Eleven
The First Asset Class—Real Estate

elen's question to Fred was, "What am I supposed to know about those Five Asset Classes [real estate, education, paper, things you can touch, and a business that you own]?"

Fred's answer was simple: "Lots. Your future, Helen, depends on your being well informed."

"But that takes work," Helen whined. "I've got my teaching and my partying time with my friends and my house cleaning and my recreation and vacation time and my yoga classes and my nap times and my . . ."

Fred held up his hand. Helen was starting to sound like most people. And most people, even in this richest country in the world, spend the last 10 or 20 years of their lives . . . poor. First, their income drops when their paycheck becomes just a pension/Social Security. Then they decide their house is "too big." What they really mean is "too expensive to keep." Then they deplete any savings they have. Then they sell the things they "don't need," which really means anything that can raise some cash. Then they consider whether their son or daughter would mind their living with them for "a while." When they are told, "Sorry, folks, we just don't have the room for you," then they think of renting out one of their spare bedrooms. They tell themselves, "Well, we never really liked going out to movies, or taking vacations, or eating out."

People in these situations do one of two things: (1) They lie to themselves to conceal the pain, or (2) live in despair.

Fred was very polite. All he said is, "I know there are a lot of things that compete for your time. All I'm saying is **if** you are going to be a bit frugal and save 25% of your income and **if** you are going to invest it wisely for the retirement years of your life, then it would make sense to learn about the Five Asset Classes rather than invest blindly. Making only 5% instead of 6% means the difference between 28.4 years to complete the pizza circle and 23.8 years. Making that extra 1% is well worth the effort."

Helen said, "I'm 19 now. Retiring in 24 years when I'm 43? I can't imagine myself being that old. I've got a job right now and things I want to do right now. I've got to get some decent drapes for my office."

They walked in different directions without saying goodbye.

Fred felt terrible. He had done his best to argue against the prevailing culture. That's really tough to do.

If everyone's drinking, you drink.

　If everyone's smoking, you smoke.

　　If everyone's watching the Super Bowl, you also watch.

　　　If everyone's got a superphone, you will get a superphone.

　　If everyone else is spending, you spend.

The more that you are like most people, the more your future will be like most people.

YUCK!*

you won't see Fred in this picture

We are talking about *your* life. When you are a kid, you obey your parents—give them what they ask. If they want you to clean your room, you do it the first time they ask.

But as an adult you don't have to do what all your friends are doing. You can if you want to, but the choice is really yours. If your real passion is studying volcanos, or playing the cello at Carnegie Hall, or being financially successful, then you will have to do what other people are not doing. And not do what other people are doing!

---

* Yuck is an expression of disgust. It entered American slang 1965–1970.

Fred headed back to his office on the third floor of the Math Building. Kingie was still painting. He painted hours each day. Over the years he had become a world-class artist. He had recently been doing a series on teddy bears.

Teddy Bear #43
$2,100

Freddy Bear
3¢

Fred knew that art wasn't his calling.

He pulled books on real estate off the shelves and stacked them on his desk.

* Some were motivational books.
* Some described how to select which real estate to buy.
* Some discussed appraising real estate.
* Some outlined the ways to borrow.
* Some showed how to fix up properties.
* Some listed the steps for advertising, showing, writing leases, collecting rents, and doing evictions.
* Some taught how to trade properties to postpone taxes.
* Some told you how to hire and supervise your apartment manager.
* Some offered an introduction in landlord-tenant law.

Fred was delighted. Most of this real estate stuff was a lot easier to understand than calculus. On the other hand, there was a lot to learn. The tax-deferred exchanges with mortgaged properties was probably the most intellectually challenging, but Fred knew that he would have to do all the other stuff—acquiring, fixing up, and running—first before he would need to think about exchanges.

Some of the books pointed to this truth: What you buy and what price you pay are major factors in what wealth you will make.

What you buy

You are buying to make money. Amateur investors love to buy pretty apartments that they can show off to their friends and brag, "Look how lovely these are!" They pay top dollar for their jewels. The price is high with respect to the rent they receive. There is little room to improve anything.

These are the people that you want to *sell* to.

The worst looking property in a half-way decent neighborhood can often be the best investment. If the previous owner hasn't picked up the trash and hasn't painted in a long time, these are encouraging signs. His price will be low (with respect to the rents) because most potential buyers want to buy "nice" properties. Picking up trash and painting are not glamorous, but they make a big difference in rents received and eventual sales price.

On the other hand, major defects, such as foundation work or extensive plumbing problems, will cost you a lot of money and might not increase the value of the property that much.

What price you pay

Prices are local. You'll never find the price of a particular property in a particular city in some book. You have to see lots of properties in order to find the best buys. Saying no to many "deals" is the road to wealth. You are not required to buy.

When to be in real estate

There is a time to be in real estate, and there is a time to get out. In 1975 (when I was a full-time college instructor), real estate wasn't that popular. I bought a pair of flats. In 1977 I bought a 32-unit place, a triplex. Then a couple of run-down houses, a 33-unit place, etc. About 70 units passed through my hands until 1980 when I got out of real estate (and teaching) and headed off to a three-story A-frame on six acres outside of Santa Rosa, California.

During those five years (1975–1980) prices were climbing. I had read a zillion books, just as Fred is doing now. I had taken eight college courses in real estate. I had done a bunch of painting as a teenager. I knew how to fill a garbage sack with trash. 1975–1980 was the right time for me to be in real estate.

On the other side of the coin, there are good times to *not* be in real estate. I had always owned the house I lived in. When I was 22 I bought my first house for $16,500. It had been vacant and bank-owned for six months. Lived there for six years, fixed it up, and sold it with a $10,000 profit. I owned the place I was living . . . in the 1960s, 1970s, 1980s, 1990s, and five years into the 2000s. Then in 2005, real estate mania had seized the nation. Housing prices were heading toward the moon. Magazine covers showed people hugging their houses. Articles were written telling people to buy now. New home builders couldn't keep up with the demand. Shortages in building materials were happening.

I sold the house I had been in for 15 years. I rented for the first time in my adult life. Reportedly, the buyer of my house sank hundreds of thousands of dollars into the place. I had a chance to look at it after he had finished remodeling. It looked gorgeous. He bought when everyone else was buying.

Three years later he listed the property for sale *at half of the amount he had paid me* . . . and it didn't sell.

One of the big advantages that real estate has over the other asset classes (education, paper, things you can touch, and a business that you own) is **leverage**.

Leverage means using debt to help buy an asset.

Let's suppose you buy an apartment house for $100,000.*

You make a 20% down payment ($20,000) and borrow the rest from a bank.

A year later you sell it for $110,000, making a $10,000 profit.

What was your rate of return? Hint: It wasn't 10%.

---

* I'm using nice round easy numbers rather than writing: "Suppose you buy an apartment house for $2,307,000." I'm also going to ignore real estate commissions and other costs. They are not relevant to the big point I'm trying to make.

You invested $20,000 of your own money and made $10,000. That's a return of 50% per year. Leverage—using borrowed money—is what made the difference.

The *Retire in 24 Years* in the previous chapter was based on the assumption of a 6% return per year.

IS THE HOME YOU LIVE IN A REAL ESTATE INVESTMENT?

Yes. That first house I bought for $16,500 had a down payment of 5% since I was buying it from the bank (and they wanted to get rid of it). The $10,000 profit over 6 years (plus six years of living at the house) was a very nice return.

Houses since WWII have often climbed in price (except for times like 2005 when they fell horribly) and the commonly accepted wisdom is that owning the house you live in is a good investment.

No. Houses, like cars, typically decline in their desirability. Older houses often have just one bathroom. Their old steel plumbing tends to clog up with rust and gunk. Their old electrical wiring (and fuses) don't fit the needs of a household today. Old roofs, termites and dry rot, windows with wood frames—the list goes on and on.

This might come as a shock, but the main reason you buy a house is to make it your home. You spend part of the 75% of your income to buy yourself shelter. Part of the 25% you are investing in the Five Asset Classes should not be diverted to home expenses.

❀   ❀   ❀

You ask, "Do I buy . . .
single family houses and rent them out,
single family houses, fix them up, and sell them,
apartment houses,
commercial real estate (stores, warehouses), or
farmland?"
If you let your pencil and your calculator discuss this on a piece of paper, they can decide which of these alternatives offers the best total return. Just give them all the data (current prices, rents, and so on).

Chapter Twelve
The Second Asset Class—Education

F red didn't have to invest many dollars in his education. In order to teach mathematics at KITTENS, he needed to know . . . mathematics. He learned his mathematics by reading. Just reading. It is probably the fastest way to learn most things.

Before he was employed Fred could comfortably get in five hours of reading each day—two in the morning, two in the afternoon, and one at bedtime. If, instead, he had attended classes, he would have to get dressed, commute to class, sit there while the teacher taught either too quickly or too slowly, do homework—some of which was too easy—and take tests. He could learn more in five hours of reading than in eight hours of running around on a campus doing the "college" stuff.

Reading is much cheaper than attending a university. For Stanford University, the current (2013–2014) tuition is $42,690 for fall/winter/spring (not including summer sessions). Housing, health care fees, and books are extra.

Their current catalog of math courses includes:

MATH 70SI: The Game of Go: Strategy, Theory, and History
Strategy and mathematical theories of the game of Go, with guest appearance by a professional Go player.

MATH 78SI: Speedcubing: History, Theory, and Practice
History of the Rubik's cube; the current cubing community; basic mathematical theory; concepts to improve speed solving skill. Prior ability to solve cube not required.

There are seven advantages to going to college over being an autodidact (= someone who learns a lot on their own).

College advantage #1: If you are unable to learn without someone forcing you, college is great. They will assign you homework. They will make you take tests. They will threaten to flunk you if you don't work.

College advantage #2: You get to sit in classrooms every day with numerous handsome/pretty members of the opposite sex. A great opportunity to say hello.

College advantage #3: You get to go to football games. This might sound fatuous, but ask college graduates about their fondest memories of their college years. More of them will mention "that great football game we won" than the day in the history class when the professor droned on about the Napoleonic wars.

College advantage #4: You get to leave home (Translation: They are not watching you as closely), and yet you can come home when you want to, so that your mom can doing your washing. Joining the army also allows you to leave home, but your sergeant will be watching you as closely as mom ever did, and you don't get to go home whenever you want to.

College advantage #5: College offers degrees. This makes it easier for employers to discriminate among the applicants. By requiring a bachelor of arts degree (B.A.), an employer can skip doing some of the testing and interviewing. If you have a B.A. stamped on your head, you are certified for some jobs.

College advantage #6: The world can be a scary place. College can be a continuation of life in the womb that is called high school. Sit in a class of several hundred* and you can hide. The world can't pick on you. You don't have to go up to a potential employer and say, "I'm good. Hire me." All you have to do is the homework and a half-way decent job on the exams and you can drift on for four (or more) years.

College advantage #7: You can get student loans to help pay for the (outrageous) costs of tuition and textbooks. You don't have to start paying the loans back until you graduate. A generation or two ago, it was not uncommon to work your way through college. Today, that is almost

---

* It isn't unusual for many of the freshman classes at a university to be very large and impersonal. Many of the freshman and sophomore classes aren't taught by those world-famous professors that the university likes to brag about. They are taught by graduate students.

impossible. Many students incur tens of thousands of dollars of student loan debt that they have to pay off

> —whether or not they graduate
> —whether or not they find a decent paying job
> —whether or not they go bankrupt. (Under current law, even if you declare bankruptcy, you can't get rid of your student loans. The loans are tattooed on the palms of your hands.)

In order to be fair, it's only right that we mention some reasons why you should *not* go to college. If your parents are insisting that you go to college, please don't read these paragraphs. It might make them angry.

(Stop reading now.) First of all, you will lose four years of income while you are attending Party Time University. Actually, that is not quite true. Two of my relatives (in the generation that followed me) took six years to graduate.

Second, the world has changed GREATLY in the last five years. When universities first began about a thousand years ago, hearing a lecture was about the only way to receive an education. When Johannes Gensfleisch Gutenberg invented printing using moveable type in the 1400s, being lectured to (rather than reading) became a luxury for the rich. Very recently, the Internet has started to offer some of the world's best teachers with much better illustrations than anything a college professor could stick on a blackboard and it's all free. The teachers are much more alive and exciting than those you'd find in the usual college classroom. And many of the online courses offer homework and exams if you need the motivation.

The people that urge you to go to college will tell you that your college education will yield lifelong dividends. That's not true in today's world. Tom Georgens, the Chief Executive Officer of NetApp (a $6.3 billion company), argues: "I know this irritates a lot of people, but once someone is at a certain point in his or her career—and it's not that far out, maybe five years—all the grades and academic credentials in the world don't mean anything anymore. It's all about accomplishment from that point on." (FORBES, December 16, 2013, p. 46)

The university that I, your author, attended back in the 1960s had a lovely campus. A stream ran through it and there were many pathways and bridges. The buildings were varied and beautiful. And there was a pizza place on the south side of campus where my wife and I went. Today that pizza place is closed. Today the institution of the physical university is going the way of the typewriter, the video cassette recorder, and the record player. Some of the big universities (Stanford, MIT, Yale, Cal) will last for another hundred years. They will remain a haven for those who want to boast, "I went to LaDeeDa University. I made a lot of connections there. My father went there, and so did his father. Blah. Blah. Blah." (You can start reading again.)

Because education is listed as one of the Five Asset Classes, it doesn't mean that education = going to class. Education means learning stuff. And this can be very financially rewarding (as well as emotionally rewarding).

When you invest in any of the other four asset classes (real estate, paper, things you can touch, and a business that you own), your education can make a big difference between returns of 18% per year and losing your shirt.

My education only began in the classroom years. After being released from teachers/home work/tests/grading I was free to learn in a more natural, productive way. (Think about it. Does sitting in a room with 25 other young people and listening to some guy talk for an hour on Monday, Wednesday, and Friday for 15 weeks seem natural to you?)

How do little kids learn? They get fascinated with something (plastic blocks or toy trucks) and play and play and play with them. Then they switch to something else. I learn like a little kid. I find an author that I like and read all his/her stuff. I fall in love with genetics and learn a lot about it. I learn all about digital photography and then move on to learn about video poker. (I live in Nevada.) After my winnings exceeded my loses by more than $20,000, I moved on to digging holes and planting fruit trees. (I've planted more than 200 of them on my land.) Education remains fun when you do it that way.

Chapter Thirteen
The Third Asset Class—Paper

E ducation for Fred was very real. He had lived in that world from the day he was born.* Owning a rental house, owning things you can touch (such as gold), owning a business—these you can put your hands on.

Paper assets feel different. You can choose your adjective: airy, ethereal, ghostlike, insubstantial.

STOCKS

Stocks mean ownership in someone else's company. You buy shares in the company. If you look in the newspaper or on the Internet you can find the price of a share of stock for many different companies.

Some stocks sell for $5 a share and others for $5,000 a share. Some companies make shoes and others do shipping. The price of a stock might be $5 one minute and $5.10 (or $4.76) the next.

In the old days, when you bought some shares, they would send you a certificate stating that you owned, say, 300 shares of the Fluffy Pineapples company. Nowadays you don't even get certificates. Your purchase is recorded on a computer somewhere.

a fluffy pineapple

There are two reasons to own 300 shares of Fluffy Pineapples. First, if the company makes money, they sometimes send part of the money to the shareholders of the company. That's called declaring a dividend. You might receive 25¢ or $3 for each share you own. It depends on the particular company. Second, if you buy 300 shares of Fluffy Pineapples at $5 a share and sell them two years later at $7 a share, you've made $600. And you've never had to hold a fluffy pineapple in your hands during those two years.

---

* Honest. On the first day the stork delivered Fred to Mr. and Mrs. Gauss, he was learning the concept of a function. (First page of the first chapter of *Life of Fred: Calculus*.)

What you gain in selling is what someone else loses. What you lose is what someone else gains. It is like being in a giant poker game. Some of the people in the stock market "game" have been playing for decades. You are playing against them. Reading only three or four books about the stock market will not make you a pro.

Stock brokers are the people you pay in order to buy or sell stocks. You can find many of them online. Some charge more than others. Some will give you tips and pointers to help you pick a stock—and will charge you extra. There are lots of places to get tips and pointers that don't cost so much—such as books and other online sites.

BONDS

A company, such as Fluffy Pineapple, might need to raise some money in order to buy more pineapple land. Instead of borrowing from a bank, they borrow from you. You might buy a Fluffy Pineapple bond for $1,000 that earns 4% per year and pays you back in, say, five years.

The same stock broker that sells you stocks, can also sell you bonds.

Instead of buying a bond directly from Fluffy, you can also buy bonds from other people who want to sell their bonds before the payoff date. The bond they originally bought might have been for $1,000 payable in five years and had an interest rate of 4%. Today there might be three years left until payoff and you want to get an effective rate of 5%. Using formulas like the ones in the Little Chapter of Horrors (Chapter 5) might help you figure out what you want to offer the bond seller.

There are two dangers in buying a bond. First, the company might go bankrupt. Second, is the danger of **inflation**.

Time Out!

Inflation happens when the government prints more paper (fiat) dollars. Inflation is an increase in the supply of money.

Since only the government can create hundred dollar bills, it is not difficult to guess who to blame for inflation.

Suppose the government inflates the money supply and suddenly everyone has ten times as much cash as they had before. Everyone might *feel* richer, but they wouldn't be, because all the prices and wages would also rise by about tenfold.

Did you know that at cup of coffee in a restaurant used to cost a dime?

Inflation (increasing the money supply) *causes* prices to rise. But inflation is not the rise in prices.

Governments with fiat currencies love to inflate. They are the first to spend the new money into the economy, and they haven't had to do the unpopular thing of raising taxes. Then the new money dilutes the value of everyone's savings. Dimes don't buy cups of coffee anymore. Government inflation becomes an almost invisible tax on every saver. It also is a painful tax on people on fixed incomes, such as retired folk on pensions.

The government will try to shift the blame for inflation to others. They might claim that some union's demands for higher wages caused prices to rise. Suppose, for example, that the union of shoemakers threatening to strike causes the employers to give the shoemakers a 10% increase in wages. If the employers are to stay in business, they will have to increase the prices of the shoes that they sell.

The government will scream, "They caused inflation!" This is a lie. First of all, the increase in prices is not inflation; it is caused by inflating the money supply. Second, with a fixed amount of fiat money in circulation, the higher prices of shoes will mean that there is less money to buy socks (and milk and cars and televisions).

The prices of all the non-shoe things will each have to fall (slightly) to compensate for the rise in shoe prices.

If the amount of money in circulation stays constant, all prices and wages couldn't rise year after year. It would be like grabbing your ankles and pulling yourself up into the air.

So if you buy a $1,000 bond that pays off in 15 years so that you can pay for your kid's college education, that $1,000 might buy one textbook. You think I'm kidding. That first house I bought for $16,500 (mentioned back in Chapter 11) had four bathrooms.

MORTGAGES

Few financial books talk about mortgages as an investment asset. It's not something that people can invest in as easily as stocks or bonds.

A central theme for successful investing is taking the unpopular path. If all the sheeple are selling, you buy. If all the sheeple are buying, you sell.

Old timers used to express that as, "Buy when there is blood in the streets. Sell when peace breaks out."

For about 15 years after I retired from teaching and owning real estate, I invested in mortgages. I lent money to people who couldn't get loans from a bank. Because of their bad credit rating or because of financial setbacks (job loss or medical problems), these borrowers were often in danger of losing their homes in foreclosure.

I could offer what few other people could offer:

✓ I had the money to lend.

✓ I knew about notes and deeds of trust from my real estate education.

✓ I knew how to fix up places in case I had to foreclose on the loan.

✓ I knew the math so that each month I could compute the principle, interest and remaining balance on each loan I made.

People were very grateful that I was there to help them. *Very grateful* translated into loans at . . . 16%. When you can offer something valuable and unique, expect to be compensated appropriately.*

When the game changed (the real estate market softened, government regulations became more onerous, and the demand for high-risk loans lessened), I stopped investing in mortgages.

REITS

You want to own real estate but don't want to have tenants calling you on Saturday saying that their toilet had backed up? A **R**eal **E**state **I**nvestment **T**rust allows you to own real estate without being a landlord. A REIT will buy a bunch of real estate. It could be shopping centers, apartment houses, or warehouses—or a mix of them. There are lots of REITs. You pick which REIT you like and purchase it through a stock broker. Your money is lumped with a zillion others. Just like owning shares in a company, you have no real control over the day-to-day operations of a REIT. The REIT pays people to buy and sell the properties and to manage the properties.

Advantages: Clean hands. You put money in and get money out. REITs can buy whole shopping centers, which you might not be able to afford on your own. You can sell your investment in a REIT faster than you can sell some real estate that you own.

---

* If all you can offer a prospective employer is your ability to walk around and smile, expect to be compensated appropriately.

Disadvantages: You are paying others to do work that you might be able to do. Doing my own painting and collecting the rents when I was first starting out in real estate saved me a bunch of money.

THREE "GLAMOROUS" REAL ESTATE INVESTMENTS

A second home, time shares, and limited partnerships all offer big psychological payoffs. To tell your friends that you own a second home in the mountains of Colorado can be a big ego trip. You tell them, "Oh, we zip on over to our mountain retreat and experience the beauty and the quiet."

Truth: No zip for a four-hour car trip. The thing remains unused except for four visits a year. It's a pain to rent it out. It would be cheaper to stay at super-luxury motels for those four visits a year. But then, of course, you couldn't brag.

Time shares are another expensive way to spend your vacation money. You buy, say, the right to use a fancy spot for the third week in October of each year. In essence you own 1/52 of the property. Time shares are often difficult to sell and because of that the salesmen collect large commissions. The maintenance costs include cleaning up after each of the 52 families spends its week there. If you want to sell your time share you might only get a fraction what you paid.

Limited partnerships mean that you stick in your money and the general partners do all the deciding. Fees and management costs can be high. It's usually really tough to find someone to sell your position to.

CERTIFICATES OF DEPOSIT

You lend money to the bank. (That sounds weird, doesn't it?) The interest they pay you is low so that they can make money lending your money out to other people. If your goal is to retire in 24 years, this is not the place to park your money.

MUTUAL FUNDS

Instead of buying individual stocks or bonds, you can put your money into a mutual fund that, in turn, buys many different stocks and/or bonds. The managers who run the mutual fund will do the work of picking out which things to invest in and which things to sell. Some managers do well some years. Others do well other years. All of them charge for their work.

Some mutual funds will announce that they've made 11% in the last year. And next year they might lose 13%.

Some invest only in United States companies. Others invest in markets around the world. Some only invest in other mutual funds!

It's been a while since we've had a *Your Turn to Play*. Please write your answers down before you turn the page and look at my work. You will learn a lot more if you do that.

Your Turn to Play

1. You buy a $500,000 apartment house. You make a down payment of $100,000 and borrow the rest of the purchase price from a bank. Make the appropriate entries into . . .

Income	Expenses
Assets	Liabilities

2. Your net worth is defined as Assets minus Liabilities. How did your net worth change after you bought the $500,000 apartment house (in the previous question)?

3. In the first year you own the $500,000 apartment house, what changes in your Income/Expenses/Assets/Liabilities might you expect?

4. Some U.S. universities are on the semester system: two semesters (Fall and Spring), each with 15 weeks of instruction.

About 20% of the U.S. universities are on the quarter system: three quarters (Fall, Winter, Spring), each with 10 weeks of instruction.

Either way, you pay your tuition and get about 30 weeks of instruction. A normal college load is 15 units, which means 15 hours of instruction per week.

As mentioned in Chapter 12, the current annual tuition for Stanford is $42,690. It's time for you to do the math. How much are they charging you per hour to sit in a class with 30 (or 400) students?

.......COMPLETE SOLUTIONS.......

1.

Income	Expenses
Assets +500,000 apartment house −$100,000 cash	Liabilities $400,000 mortgage

2. Your assets increased by $400,000 (The math: 500,000 − 100,000).
    Your liabilities increased by $400,000.
    Your net worth changed by $0 (The math: 400,000 − 400,000).

3. You can expect your income to increase because of the rents you collect.

    You can expect your expenses to increase because of property taxes, insurance, maintenance of the building, interest paid on the mortgage, increased income taxes, business license, eviction expenses. . . .

    You hope that income > expenses, which will mean that you will be able to put cash in the bank. Your assets will increase.

    The building might increase in value, which will also increase your assets.

4. Computing the cost/hour to sit in a Stanford classroom can be eye opening.

    Thirty weeks times 15 hours/week = 450 hours of instruction/year.

$$\begin{array}{r} 94.86 \\ 450\overline{)42690.00} \\ \underline{4050} \\ 2190 \\ \underline{1800} \\ 3900 \\ \underline{3600} \\ 3000 \\ \underline{2700} \end{array}$$

$42,690 divided by 450

$94 an hour to receive group instruction! This is insane.

Chapter Fourteen
The Fourth Asset Class—Things You Can Touch

Fred has never really thought about retiring. He loves teaching too much. But the idea of becoming financially independent in 24 years by investing in assets that grow by 6% per year really excites him.

If KITTENS University went bankrupt 25 years from now (when Fred is 31), he could offer to teach at another university for free or travel around the world or be a full-time dad to his kids.* A number of universities do shut down each year.

What if I bought stuff? he thought to himself. He had read somewhere that a guy had bought baseball cards and had made a fortune when he sold them. He had read about a woman who bought paintings and made a fortune when she sold them. He had read about a man who collected antique chairs and had made a fortune when he sold them.

"Life After Drugs"
by Alfred Thimbletwerp

These three stories might be true, but they are extremely rare events. These three people have been extremely lucky. Setting out to make a killing in baseball cards has about the same chance of success as heading to Hollywood in hopes of becoming a movie star. It happens, but it's a one-in-a-million shot. If you want to buy an antique chair, do it because it gives you pleasure to own it—not for the thought of making a buck.

_____

* Fred sometimes thinks about having children. He imagines that they would be more fun than dogs or cats. He thought *If I had eight kids, I could name them One, Two, Three, Four, Five, Six, Seven, and Eight. That would be so cool. Then I could say, "Odd ones do the dishes. Even ones mop the floors." That would save a lot of time.*

At the age of 6, he didn't give too much thought to romance. He had gone through a "romantic period" in *Life of Fred: Geometry,* but that didn't turn out too well. He's still recovering. When Fred becomes a teenager, thoughts of romance might again enter his head.

Fred likes to collect bow ties. He just likes them. He has more than he will ever be able to wear out in a dozen lifetimes. It's okay. Anybody who saves 80% of their income can buy bottle caps or used shoelaces if they wish.

I, your author, love fountain pens. I like the way they feel when I write with them. I got one from my mother when she died, and over the years I have bought a bunch more. Nothing super expensive—usually in the $6–$60 range. (There are lots of fountain pens in the $600 range, but they have no appeal to me.) And I buy bottles of ink—a different color for each pen.

Fred isn't buying bow ties and I'm not buying fountain pens as investments. We are spending our money *for pleasure*, which is one very good use of money after you have set aside your 25% for savings.

One big problem with collectibles (stamps, comic books, art work, rare books, diamonds, fur coats) is that their value depends so much on what seems to be popular right now. Fur coats were very popular in the 1930s, but who wears them now? Autographs of Roy Rogers and Dale Evans? Some people (whose childhood wasn't in the 1950s) might not even know who they are.

Invest in bananas? Buy two thousand dollars worth of bananas this week and tell me how much they'll be worth in a month?

Invest in sheets of plywood? Buy two thousand dollars worth and in ten years it might be worth about two thousand dollars, but where are you going to store it? The storage costs for those ten years might be two thousand dollars.

The trouble with diamonds and other gems is that the buying price is much higher than the selling price. Buy a diamond for $10,000 and you might have a tough time finding anyone who will pay you $8,000 for it. Diamonds, like real estate, are not a very liquid investment. They're easy to buy and hard to sell.

Gold and silver? A definite maybe. The buying prices and the selling prices are close to each other. They are easily bought and sold. Where they really shine is in their ability to store value. An ounce of gold in 1900 bought a very fine man's suit. An ounce of gold today buys a very fine man's suit. Paper dollars (fiat currency) is a lousy store of value. Inflation drives the purchasing power of a buck downward each year. A pre-1965 quarter (which is 90% silver) can buy a gallon of gas today.

Chapter Fifteen
The Fifth Asset— Your Own Business

There are a thousand different ways that parents rear* their kids. If your dad is a rodeo star, he might teach you a lot of ways to stay on a bucking horse. If your parents own a funeral home, you might learn a lot about undertaking as you grow up.

Some parents are very happy if their child decides to follow in their footsteps. If the sign over the shop reads, they might be very happy if someday it reads

> John Henry
> Blacksmith

> John Henry
> and son
> Blacksmiths

Some parents hope their children become lawyers or doctors. They imagine bragging, "My son became an attorney. My daughter is an internist at Mighty Med hospital.**"

Fred's parents (Mr. and Mrs. Gauss) took a different approach. They didn't care. His father watched television and took month-long trips to Save-the-Something conferences. His mother baked cookies while Fred played on the kitchen floor. Fred even had to change his own diapers until he read Prof. Eldwood's *Potty Training for Your Child*.

---

* In the U.S. both *rear your children* and *raise your children* are commonly used. In dictionaries the first meaning of *rear* is to bring up children. It's usually about the seventh definition of *raise* that gets to that meaning. Diction (= good choice of words) is important for a writer. Diction says use *broken* rather than *busted*.

** Lawyer or doctor? A generation ago these might have been very desirable occupations. Currently, in many places there is an oversupply of lawyers, and those that find a position in a law firm often have to work very long hours. Many doctors have been retiring early rather than continuing their career under the heavy hand of government.

What are the common messages that parents give their kids? When mom puts daughter to bed at night, they might talk about the daughter becoming a dancer or of finding a wonderful husband ("a prince") who is both sober and wealthy. A son might be pushed to go to college and then be employed by MegaSuper Corp. "Some day, son," he is told, "you will be president of MegaSuper Corp."

Here is the *un*common message: "I want the best for you. I don't want you to be employed. I want you to employ others. I don't want you to be owned by some corporation. I want you to own it. I want you to become a businessman/businesswoman."

This is a message that very few kids hear. Being your own boss is probably the most certain road to real wealth. But very few Americans take that path.

If you are not going to spend all your income (like most Americans do), then you have a choice among Five Asset Classes:

A) real estate
B) education
C) paper
D) things you can see and touch
E) your own business.

When six-year-old Fred read this list, he had several thoughts:

Regarding real estate . . .

The government won't let me sign a contract to buy any real estate until I'm older. I also haven't saved enough to make a down payment on any real estate yet. In addition, I have a lot more books on real estate that I want to read before I get my first property.

My other thought is that whoever made this list might have made a slight error. If you buy houses to rent, apartments, or commercial property and you manage it yourself, then it is a business, not just an investment. It's not like buying a CD (certificate of deposit) and just waiting until it matures.

Regarding education . . .

My reading, which has been my education, allowed me to get my teaching job at KITTENS. Savings from my salary allows me to invest in the Five Asset Classes.

Small Time Out

For most people, the road to retirement in 24 years begins by being employed and saving 25% of their salary.

For the lucky few who have parents who themselves have done the saving and investing, financial help from parents might shorten the time before moving from salaried to full-time business owner.

Regarding paper investments . . .

If I invest my savings in stocks, bonds, mortgages, and so on, then someday I'm gonna get paid . . . in paper. With the real danger of high inflation (because of government printing of currency), all my savings might only buy a doughnut.

Inflation Happens

In this country in November 1974, the annual rate of inflation was 12.3%.

In March 1980, the annual rate was 14.8%.

The real horror story was in Germany in the early 1920s. In 1919 the German dollar—called a mark—was worth about 24 cents. You could exchange 4.2 marks for a U.S. dollar.

In 1922, it took 400 marks to buy a dollar. In three years a mark had lost 99% of its purchasing power. Then things got worse. On November 15, 1923, it took 1,300,000,000,000 marks to buy a buck. That's 1.3 trillion marks.

On the next day, it took 4.3 trillion marks to buy a dollar. People had wheelbarrows full of currency with which they could buy a piece of gum.

People who had a million marks in their bank accounts in 1919, couldn't buy a toothpick four years later with their savings. The middle class was wiped out. Historically, when there is no middle class, dictators often arise.

Regarding things you can see and touch . . .

Gold and silver could protect me against hyperinflation. Online I can purchase pre-1965 silver dimes and quarters. They are sold in bags of $1,000 face value. That would be 10,000 dimes. If paper money became worthless, silver dimes might be used as money.

Without silver and gold, we might have to resort to a barter economy—trading things. I want to sell my refrigerator. Someone offers me their superphone plus four chickens. I already have two superphones, so I trade the extra superphone for 180 cans of green beans. I trade the four chickens for a yard of silk cloth.
I trade 40 cans of green beans and the silk cloth for a ukelele.
I don't know how to play a ukelele. All I know is that it's a great word in Scrabble™ if you have lots of e's.

ukelele

Regarding investing in my own business . . .

This, Fred thought, looks like it has the best potential to make 6% per year. While I'm selecting which business to get into and preparing myself for that business, I'll park my savings in stocks or silver.

Chapter Sixteen
Growing Your Business

F red sat at his desk in his office. He watched Kingie quietly painting. Kingie had found his calling in life and he happily worked hour after hour. In the first couple of years, he learned more and more about oil painting. In the third year, he sold several of his paintings for $49. Now his paintings routinely sell for two or three thousand dollars apiece. He has hired a man who comes to Kingie's Art Studio (which is a corner of Fred's office) each day to pick up paintings and take them to the Kingie Art Gallery to be displayed.

He has also hired a webmaster who maintains the Kingie Art Website. The website has photos of the available paintings, their prices, and how to order them. As the orders come in, the webmaster passes them along to the Kingie Art Distribution Manager who removes the paintings from the Kingie Art Gallery, packages them, and ships them. Packaging the paintings is especially difficult because many of them haven't had a chance to dry yet.

One key to business success is to concentrate on the part where you are irreplaceable.

When Kingie was first starting out in his oil painting business, he had to do everything himself. That is the natural way to begin. But if your business is to really grow, at some point you have to let go of some of the tasks that others can do more cheaply than you.

Many business owners never graduate to that second step.

The math is really simple. When Kingie is painting, he can usually do about one picture an hour. This makes, say, $2,300 per hour. If he stops painting and spends time hanging paintings at the Kingie Art Gallery, he is making $40 per hour. But, in effect, he is losing $2,260 an hour. (The math: $40 - 2,300 = -2,260$)

When you open your new business—Waddles Doughnuts—you will make the doughnuts, serve the customers, do the bookkeeping, sweep the floors, and clean the bathrooms. New business owners often put in 60-hour work weeks doing all the aspects of the business. There is nothing unusual with that.

The big error happens when you don't let go of things as Waddles Doughnuts becomes more popular. It might be really fun for you to mix the dough, shape it into ◉'s, plop them into the grease, and watch them turn golden brown. But if that's why you created the Waddles Doughnuts business, you are an idiot. It would be a lot easier just to get employed by Blubo Doughnuts (the doughnut shop down the street) and just make doughnuts eight hours a day. Then you would have all the joy of doughnut making (for the next 40 years of your life) and none of the hassles of business ownership.

In the earliest years of your Waddles Doughnuts business, you might be sweeping the floors. **Cash flow** (income minus expenses) is very important to watch. You probably won't have much startup capital and during the first year or so, your cash flow will probably be negative. It will be eating into your startup capital. Many new businesses die because of overspending. Buying the computer and office furniture can make a much bigger dent in your capital than renting or leasing them.

When you can be doing something that brings in more than your sweeping the floor at $8/hour, then you get someone else to sweep the floors.
That's the secret of knowing when to let go.

You either hire a sweeper or you outsource the work to a company that does sweeping. Doing the math will tell you which is cheaper.

Chapter Seventeen
Hiring

F red was pretty good at math (an understatement), but computing how much hiring someone would really cost was nearly impossible. Government taxes and regulations made solving $\int_{x=a}^{b} \sec^2 x\, dx$ look like child's play.*

You start with their base pay, say, $8/hour.

Then you have to get workers compensation insurance.

Then there are forms to fill out regarding their number of dependents and proof that you must gather to show that they are legally allowed to work (such as proof of citizenship).

Then with each paycheck you have to make mandatory deductions for Social Security, government medical program(s), income tax deductions, and unemployment program(s).

At the very least, you have to file 15 forms each year and often have to kick in additional money of your own in addition to the money you've withheld from the employee. In a state with state income tax there will be additional deductions and additional forms to submit.

Sometimes you might see someone beside the road holding a sign that reads, "Will work for food." The government has made it impossible for you to legally trade his mowing your lawn for a hot meal. Besides determining the value of that meal for income tax purposes, you would have to do all the stuff (get workers compensation insurance, have him present proof of citizenship, somehow make deductions for all the categories and submit the forms to the county, state and federal agencies, etc.) Remember to laugh when some government official claims that he is all in favor of fostering full employment.

Suppose your Waddles Doughnuts has prospered and you have eight stores scattered around the county. You need someone to sweep those eight stores each night and clean the bathrooms. It's not hard to contact janitorial service companies and find out how much it would cost to hire one of their employees. The real question is whether you should

---

* It is child's play. It's equal to tan b – tan a.

hire someone who would be a Waddles employee instead of outsourcing that work.

Here's the handy rule-of-thumb:

Hire someone only if they will increase the company's net earnings by at least seven times their base salary.

If a potential employee's base salary for doing janitorial work for you is $8/hour, then the magic number is $56/hour.

If you are the owner of Waddles Doughnuts and you can spend your time getting a ninth store established (and your time doing that will net the company $100/hour), then you hire an employee to sweep and clean.

If you are the owner and your efforts can only yield an increase in net earnings of $50/hour, then you clean the bathrooms rather than hiring the $8/hour employee.

❀   ❀   ❀

Right now, only 47% of adult Americans have a full-time job.

Right now 6,000,000 Americans in the 16- to 24-year-old age aren't in school and aren't working.

Recently, Wal-Mart opened up two new stores. They were offering 600 jobs. More than 23,000 people applied.

$$
\begin{array}{r}
38 \\
600{\overline{\smash{\big)}\,23000}} \\
\underline{1800} \\
5000 \\
\underline{4800} \\
\end{array}
$$

More than 38 applicants for each Wal-Mart job.

You can be and should be very picky about whom you hire.

Chapter Eighteen
Employ or Be Employed

Fred sat at his desk and tried to map out his future. He started with the math: he figured that he had about 700,000 hours* left to live. He wanted to live deliberately, rather than just wandering through life doing stuff.

He didn't want his tombstone to look like this:

Here lies
Fred Gauss

Born,
watched TV,
shopped,
and died.

What Fred discovered is that it is very hard to predict ahead five years.

This is true when you are 6.

This is true when you are 12.

This is true when you are 20.

This is true when you are 40.

This is true when you are 70.

When you are 20, you don't know whether a Great Romance is just around the corner. When you are 70, you don't know whether you should be ordering your tombstone yet. One friend of mine was to be married in a couple of weeks. Her mom woke her up early one morning to tell her that her fiancé died in a car accident during the night.

It's almost as if we live in a world filled with fog and can only see clearly a couple of feet ahead of us. Despite that, we have to make long-term decisions as to whom to marry, what field to study, what business to begin. It's not fair, but it *is* reality.

We can't lift the fog, but with effort we can see a little bit further. Here's how you can make the effort:

---

* 80 years × 365 days/year × 24 hours/day = 700,800 hours, which rounds to 700,000 hours. This was just a rough estimate. He didn't have to consider leap years and other details.

✳ Get to know the person you are thinking of marrying. Choosing the right person can make a big difference in your happiness for the next 50 years. You don't want to find out *after* you are married that he/she doesn't want any children (and you want six).

✳ The first two years of college often expose the student to English, history, a lab science, music, a foreign language, political science, and physical education in fencing, tennis, or jazz dancing.

Read books in many different fields.

Talk to people about their jobs.

Discover what kinds of things excite *you*. They will probably be different than what excites your friends.

Fred sat at his desk thinking about his future. He knew that mathematics excited him. But how that might be expressed in his life is a different question. He is a university professor right now. Some day his love of math might be expressed in

making math movies,

writing *Life of Stan* math books,

in a profession that uses a lot of math,* or

in a business he owns that could use his math talents.

Wait a minute! I, your reader, need to break in here for a moment. Three chapters ago you wrote about "Your Own Business." Two chapters ago the title was "Growing Your Business." The previous chapter was "Hiring."

Aren't you making a tiny **assumption that I'm going to own a business? I want to hear both sides of the debate: Being employed vs. being an employer.**

But there are three sides to this debate. You don't just have choice of getting a job or going into business.

Three sides? You never mentioned three sides.

---

* For example, actuaries, architects, chemists, computer systems analysts, cryptologists, economists, geologists, geophysicists, oceanographers, meteorologists, operations research analysts, physicists, astronomers, robotics engineers, statisticians.

But there are three sides. If you, my reader, want me to talk about your real alternatives, there are three of them. Getting a job (the most popular). Getting welfare (the second most popular). Owning a business (the least popular).

Okay. Let the debate begin!

(the first speaker) Getting a job.

There are many advantages to having a job. You get a salary. You know what it's going to be. It's a lot more money than being on welfare. It is much more certain than operating a business.

Your hours are fixed and you get to go home at night and forget about what you did during the day. If you own a business, you often will work 12 hours/day and will be thinking about your business all the time.

You know when your vacations are coming.

You don't have to work that hard (unless you are paid on commission). If you make mistakes, your employer has to pay for them.

In many jobs, such as at Waddles Doughnuts, your employer will furnish you with a snappy-looking uniform.

You will be covered by workers compensation insurance in case you fall into the boiling doughnut grease at Waddles.

If you talk with fellow employees of the same sex as you are, there will probably be few rules about what you can say.

You will be given a guaranteed break, say, 15 minutes every four hours.

Your take-home salary (which will be about 60% of your gross salary after federal and state income taxes, Social Security, unemployment insurance, etc. is removed) is yours every week.*

If you want more salary, all you have to do is beg for it. You might get a raise unless, of course, there are 38 other people ready to take your job at your current salary.

If you are working in a field in which you might someday start a business, having a job is a great way to: ① find out if you like that kind of business, and ② learn the good and bad ways to run that business.

---

* Unless your boss says two magic words: "You're fired."

(the second speaker) Get Welfare.

You don't need to make eye contact with anyone. No boss to please. No customers to please.

You can throw away your alarm clock.

No stupid income tax forms to fill out.

You can watch television during the daytime.

If you want extra money, you don't have to ask for a raise. You do things for other people for cash—cash that doesn't get reported to the government. If some landscaping company tells an owner that they'll do the work for $100, you can offer to do it for $75 since you don't have to deal with all those government deductions. This is, of course, illegal, but people like C.C. Coalback only consider whether they will be caught, not whether it breaks a law.

Having more children doesn't cost as much as when you have a job. To start with, the more kids you have, the more welfare you receive. If you want even more money, one trick that might work is to abandon your kids to the government. Then have your mother (who has biological "rights") adopt the kids and get paid for taking care of them.

Claim you are really looking hard for work, but magically only find it when the government unemployment benefits are about to run out.

There are a million ways to make the system work for you . . . while you don't work.

This is supposedly the richest country in the world, and yet one out of every five households (20%) is on food stamps. Many people don't go to their grocery store on the first or second of each month to avoid the mobs of people with their carts filled with food paid by the taxpayers.

Why work, if by doing so, you lose your food stamps, your housing assistance, and your free medical? If for every ten dollars you earn, you lose five dollars in welfare, that's effectively a 50% tax on what you earn.

(rebuttal to the welfare speaker)

Certainly, there is a small number of people who need charity.

When the government hands out money to the needy, it is not charity no matter who receives it. One essential part of the definition of charity is that it is voluntary. The only way that government gets its money is by forcibly extracting it from the people in our society who are producers. Try not paying your taxes and you'll learn the meaning of forcible extraction. They can *take* everything valuable that you own.

Only money voluntarily donated to help the poor, whether it be personally or through churches or other associations, is true charity.

Second, the federal government cannot legally be engaged in any welfare programs (or education programs).

The Constitution specifically prohibits the federal government from messing with welfare or education. I bet this is never mentioned in the government schools! Any fifth-grader can understand the plain intended language of the Constitution.

Here it is.

Article 1, Section 8 states the 18 powers that the Congress has:

1. Lay and collect taxes
2. Borrow money
3. Regulate commerce
4. Make rules for becoming a citizen and for doing bankruptcies
5. Coin money and determine weights and measures
6. Punish counterfeiting
7. Establish post offices
8. Establish copyrights and patents for writers and inventors
9. Set up law courts below the Supreme Court
10. Punish pirates
11. Declare war
12. Raise an army
13. Raise a navy
14. Make rules governing the army and navy
15. Make rules for calling up a militia
16. Make rules for creating a militia
17. Set up a less-than-ten-square-mile area for the federal government
18. Make any laws to carry out the powers granted by the first 17 powers.

Do you see any powers to run welfare or education programs? And then in the Tenth Amendment (in the Bill of Rights) *specifically* states that those 18 parts of Article 1, Section 8 *are all that Congress is allowed to do.* They can't touch welfare or education.

Amendment 10: The powers not delegated to the United States by the Constitution, nor prohibited by it to the States, are reserved to the States respectively, or to the people.

The president and all the members of Congress have sworn that they will uphold the Constitution   not just promised, they swore. It is called their oath of office. To swear an oath is *not* the same as making an extra serious promise. It means to call God as your witness to the truth of what you are saying.

This was perhaps best explained in Robert Bolt's *A Man for All Seasons*. In that play (and movie) the hero explains to his daughter:

"When a man takes an oath, Meg, he's holding his own self in his own hands. Like water. And, if he opens his fingers then he needn't hope to find himself again." In other words, he is damned.

(the third speaker) Owning a business

Wow. It's easy to see why being employed or going on welfare are the two most popular choices. Only about 7% of all non-farm workers are self-employed and that number has been rapidly declining in recent years.

❑ Who in blazes wants to put in 12-hour days?

❑ Who wants to worry about paying for mistakes that your employees make?

❑ Who wants to face the risk of failure that many new businesses experience?

❑ Who wants to face the Big Enemy—government—which puts up a thousand barriers to owning and operating a business and then sucks off about 40% of the net income of successful business owners?

❑ Who wants to trade the one boss (for those who are employed) for the hundreds of bosses that every business has? As a business owner, all your customers are your bosses and they can fire you by not liking what you have to sell.

☒ The answer is: Everyone who wants to retire in 24 years.

Owning your own business is the surest way to wealth (unless you are counting on your rich uncle to leave you tons of money or you plan on marrying someone rich*).

---

* Increasingly common nowadays are prenuptial contracts, which state that after marriage each party keeps as his or her own separate property the things they had before the marriage. You won't be a dime richer by marrying The Rich One.

Chapter Nineteen
Which Business?

Fred heard the sound of a big truck pulling up to the Math Building. That was unusual. The largest vehicle that usually comes to the Math Building is the Vendy Vending Machine truck, which comes once a week to refill the nine vending machines on the third floor.

Fred headed to the window to look.

Four men got out of the truck and headed up to the second floor, to Helen's office. They were here to put in a new Italian marble fireplace.

Helen's new office fireplace—almost like Fred had imagined it

Almost immediately the pounding of large sledgehammers began. Their first step was to enlarge the window.

Fred didn't want to hear the construction noise or think about how soon Helen would be bankrupt.*

He left Kingie, who didn't seem to be bothered by the noise, and headed down the hallway past the nine vending machines—four on the left and five on the right—down two flights of stairs, past the fireplace truck, and toward Main Street.

One thought that was running through Fred's mind was what kind of business he might enjoy owning.

Enjoy owning is an important part of choosing a business. If you hate dogs, selecting a pet grooming store would be silly.

As Fred walked down Main Street, he passed Pete's Pool Hall. That didn't appeal to him at all.

---

* That would happen in December. Helen would lose everything . . . except the student loans, which can't be discharged in bankruptcy.

He passed the **Bee-Bop Bakery**. The idea of baking cookies and cakes for the next 20 years made his skin crawl. No thanks.

He realized that many businesses wouldn't be located at a retail outlet on Main Street. He looked in the phone book and found a long listing of companies that clear away junk.

Clean & Clear	Off It Goes!
Disposal of Your Doodads	Pick & Clear
Happy Haulers	Quik No Clutter
I Can Make It Clean	Rubbish Truckers
Junk Away!	Stuff Our Truck
Kitchen & Kloset Klearing	Your Stuff Becomes My Stuff
Lift & Load	Watch It Disappear
Mess No Mo'	Zoom, Boom, More Room

One important thing to remember is . . .

Don't pick a business that has a lot of competition.

If all your friends are opening antique stores, don't!

In many fields the competition is *way too intense*. Your chances of succeeding as a major league baseball player, a popular singer, or an astronaut are about the same as finding a donkey that speaks Hebrew. (That happened once in history as far as I know.)

Avoid the glamorous fields. Your goal, hopefully, is to find a business that thrives, not one that you can boast about at a party. It is okay if you choose something that would be boring to other people such as operating a landfill or manufacturing parrot cages.

Find a niche where few others can compete with your set of skills and talents.

Determining what your skills and talents are is the first step.

Do you like to hike in the woods? Do you like playing with mice? Do you read books about astronomy? In your circle of friends are you the one who often thinks of what the group can do? Do you have friends? When you think about time in the kitchen, do you imagine washing dishes or making Brie stuffed pain perdu with cranberry cherry sauce? Do you know how to tie a square knot?

All the way through your life you will discover new things that you like, but most of the main aspects of who you are will start to become evident in your teenage years.

Those *main aspects of who you are* will not point you to *a* particular business. There will always be a dozen possible businesses that would be a good fit for you.

Suppose, for example, you like walking in the woods, like time alone, and like simple cooking. Those things could point to several different directions:

A) You could be like John Muir who was famous for enjoying places like Yosemite. He would sometimes go out walking for a whole day with just a tea bag in his pocket.

B) You could be like Lewis and Clark who explored deep into the wilderness.

C) You could be an escaped convict hiding in the woods.

You can take tests that will highlight which are your strengths. (vocational tests and aptitude tests) You can talk with people in your areas of interest. Thinking, praying, daydreaming—these can all help you center down to a thought like The business of opening a school for morticians calls to me. (Your particular choice might be different!)

I, your reader, have to interrupt again. At what point in my life am I supposed to "center down," as you call it, to a particular idea? When I'm 6 (like Fred), or 16, or 26?

I am not talking about making a final choice that can't be changed. Most people do not have just a single direction in life, as Mother Teresa did, but a variety of avenues they explore.

But your question is, "When do I center down on a particular avenue?"

Right. That's my question.

You might only have 600,000 hours left to live. (Twelve years is about 100,000 hours.) When do you center down? The answer is easy: Yesterday. And if that option is not available to you, then Today is the next best choice. Tomorrow stinks as an alternative.

If the thought of manufacturing collars and leashes for ferrets is what most appeals to you right now, then this is where you start. Today.

Fred needed a quieter place to think. He jogged back onto campus and headed to the rose garden. He hopped up (rather than sat down) on one of the benches and pulled out paper and a pencil.

My Skills & Talents

1. math
2. teaching
3. I'm three feet tall. That might come in handy for working in tight spaces.
4. I'm fairly young.
5. I love to read.
6. I don't have a family.

       That's good in that I don't have people dependent on me. There are dangerous businesses that I wouldn't consider (such as minefield clearing) if I had a wife and kids.

       That's bad in that getting married and staying married is highly correlated with economic success.*

7. I am well disciplined.
8. I get along with people.
9. I am always honest.**
10. I am healthy. I like jogging.
11. I like cats and dogs but not mice.

Fred had read in a book that after looking at one's skills and talents, 𝔍oday is the time to center down—to make a tentative choice—as to what business to enter.

      Fred chose . . .

---

* Thomas J. Stanley, as reported in his book, *The Millionaire Mind,* made a survey of 733 millionaires. He asked them to rate 30 success factors and declare which ones best explained their economic success.

      Forty-nine percent responded that having a supportive spouse was "very important."

** Being honest with everyone; Being well-disciplined; Getting along with people—these were the only success factors that the 733 millionaires rated more highly than having a supportive spouse.

Chapter Twenty
The First Step after Choosing

Fred looked over his list of eleven skills and talents. The one that best described him was teacher. He knew that he wouldn't be able to find a business that exactly fit everything on his list.

He put "teacher" at the center of a page and exploded the idea.

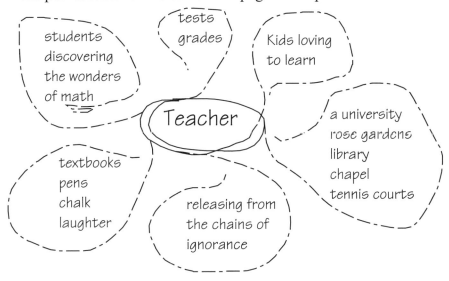

Fred chose: **I will found a university.**

That released a flood of ideas—always a good sign.

✓ My university will be inexpensive.

✓ My university will have teachers whose first love is teaching and not research or publishing.

✓ The teachers won't be paid on the basis of how old they are (like KITTENS University does). They won't be paid on the basis of how many years they've taught.

✓ This university will be a very classical university. It won't be a trade school designed for getting a job. No classes in floristry or in forestry. Each class will aim to expose the students to the very best that our civilization has to offer.

✓ Each class will show the essential inner coherence between the academic subjects—English, math, history, philosophy—in addition to emphasizing the why as much as the how.

✓ No teacher will just teach facts. Memorizing is so much less important than understanding. Therefore every exam will be open book, open notes. This will prevent teachers from doing lazy fact-teaching.

Fred was in love with the idea of starting a university.

> Small warning: No matter what you choose, there will be days ahead where you are not in love with your choice.
>
> No matter whom you marry, no matter which field you choose, no matter how real your calling in life is—there will be times where you want to chuck it all in and run away. This is natural. It happens. Don't let it freak you out.

After centering down and choosing, the next step is often the scariest: You have to reinvent who you are. (Let those words sink in for a moment.) You have to reinvent who you are.

Ouch! I, your reader, am very happy with who I am right now. I'm not in the mood to go changing myself. And "reinventing" sounds worse than just making some changes.

It is.

Am I going to lose touch with myself?

Which self? Almost all of us are changing. You aren't exactly the same person as you were yesterday. The whole goal of Fred's University, for example, is to change students. The graduating senior is to be much different than the entering freshman.

If you don't want to change, if after high school you just want to get a job to feed yourself, watch football*, and just think about the good

---

* Someone gets the ball. He either throws it, runs with it, or kicks it.

old days, you will have a lot of company . . . in the cemetery. Most people who have ever lived are dead right now. Most people who are living right now are just killing time.

Reinventing yourself is not for cowards. Being brave doesn't mean not feeling fear or pain. The brave feel the icy fingers of fear on their spines. They hurt. But they still move forward.

Reinventing yourself, if you don't dawdle, will take three or four years.

We all carry a mental business card. Yesterday, Fred's would have read: FRED GAUSS, MATH TEACHER AT KITTENS UNIVERSITY. Today, he is rewriting it:

Fred Gauss
founder of a university

Today, if you ask Fred, "Who are you?" he is learning to respond, "I am a founder of a university."

If you say, "What university? I don't see it," he will answer, "But I do."

Right now, Fred's thought of his university is just a twinkle in his eye—a foggy haze of a dream. In three or four years the reinvention of himself—that dream—will solidify and become alive. Marshmallow sauce will become stainless steel. Until you have seen this happen, it's almost impossible to describe.

Okay. I'm willing to sign up. What's next?

In three words: Five thousand hours.

Um. Could you elaborate a little?

I'd be glad to. Fred is going to live, eat, and sleep with his vision of Fred's University. He will talk with students and other faculty members about what would make a great university. He will visit other campuses. He will check online and with real estate brokers to find real estate that might be used. He will learn that some colleges go bankrupt and have an empty campus waiting to be used. He will learn about private colleges that are looking for a buyer. He will learn all about accreditation. He might go see the movie "Goodbye, Mr. Chips" (1939) and learn about school traditions. He will look at the websites of many universities. He will make lists, lots of them—courses to be taught, kinds of trees to be planted on the campus, supplies that each instructor will receive. He will draft faculty manuals, compose a university hymn, and draw sketches of the buildings.

But, most importantly, he will read. Reading is probably the best mentor. Much of those 5,000 hours will be spent reading. He will get books from the KITTENS University library, from the public library, from friends. He will buy books. One or two or three of them at a time.

He will read books about the souls of great universities,
about which private universities are prospering,
about which universities have failed,
about hiring faculty and staff,
about current trends in education,
about accreditation,
about trees and flowers on a campus,
about maintaining and renovating academic buildings,
about government laws and regulations for universities,
about university mascots,
about accounting,
about insurance,
about campus safety,
about class rings.

Inspirational books and how-to books. At least a couple hundred books.

One of two things will happen. Either Fred will discover that founding a university is not really the path for him, or he will, after 5,000 hours, find that there will be only a couple hundred people in the world who know as much as he does about founding a university.

This preparation is the essential first step for success.

If your field of interest is bowling alleys, you don't start by going out and buying a bowling alley.

Chapter Twenty-one
Sedulousness and Inexorableness

Fred put away his paper and pencil and headed back toward the Math Building. He could feel those 5,000 hours ticking away. He wanted to talk over his dream of founding a university with Kingie who is one of the most successful ~~people~~ dolls that Fred knew. He had done those years of preparation, day after day, and now Kingie was one of the top two or three hundred oil painters in the world.[*]

As Fred walked he wondered how hard it would be to amass 5,000 hours. His teaching schedule was only "slightly" longer than the average university professor's.[**] (Most of them teach 6–9 hours/week. Fred teaches 45 hours/week.)

He immediately noticed that he had a five-minute break that he could use toward his 5,000 hours. That's a start he thought to himself.

Fred's Daily Schedule
8–9 Arithmetic
9–10 Beginning Algebra
10–11 Advanced Algebra
11–noon Geometry
noon–1 Trigonometry
1–2 Calculus
2–3 Statistics
3–3:05 Break
3:05–4 Linear Algebra
4–5 Seminar in Biology, Economics, Physics, Set Theory, Topology, and Metamathematics.

As Fred walked up the two flights of stairs in the Math Building, he was computing: There are 30 weeks in an academic year. That's 150 days. During those 150 days of teaching each year, I can put in an hour in the morning (after jogging) and two hours in the evening. That's 3 × 150 = 450 hours during my teaching days. That leaves 215 days (The math: 365 - 150.) Subtract off 52 Sundays. That leaves 163 days with no teaching commitment. Ten hours a day working on my founding a university and five hours of goofing around and nine hours of sleep—any idiot could do that.

---

[*] Hey! This is really true. I challenge you to make a list of the hundred top living oil painters. I bet that even before you had listed six of them, you will have thought of Kingie.

[**] And the Pacific Ocean is only slightly wetter than popcorn.

As Fred walked past the nine vending machines, he added up the numbers: 450 hours during the teaching days plus 1,630 during the non-teaching, non-Sunday days equals 2,080 hours each year to devote to getting ready to launch my university.

I had read somewhere he thought to himself that these 5,000 hours would take three or four years. That must be for slackers.

And Fred was the kind of guy who can make a schedule *and keep to it*. He was sedulous (= persevering). He had what some call *grit*. On those 163 non-teaching, non-Sunday days, no temptation could turn the five hours of goofing off into six. He was inexorable (= not to be pulled off his intended path). In fact, on many of those 163 days, he would decide to work halftime—12 hours out of every 24.

In every business adventure there is an element of luck. Fred was determined to make the element of luck as small as possible.

When Fred entered his office, it was dark. He thought Kingie must have turned off the light and gone into his fort for a little nap, but that wasn't the case. He will still doing oil paintings but was working by candlelight.

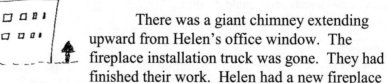

"Did the electricity go out?" Fred asked Kingie.

"No. The sun disappeared."

"That's not possible," Fred said. "I was just outside, and the sun was shining as it always does during a Kansas summer."

He looked out his office window and something big and black was obscuring the view. He ran down the hallway past the nine vending machines, down two flights of stairs and out into the sunshine. What he saw shocked him.

There was a giant chimney extending upward from Helen's office window. The fireplace installation truck was gone. They had finished their work. Helen had a new fireplace in her office. Fred's window was completely blocked by the chimney.

One of the most important skills needed for any business owner (and any parent) is the ability to solve apparently insoluble problems.

Having a chimney built right over your window is one of those apparently insoluble problems. Fred could complain to Helen, but that probably wouldn't do any good. He could talk to the university president, except that the president is on a three-month cruise.

He gave a little push on the chimney and it tilted slightly. With a couple more pushes, he could see out his window again.

This creative solution was fast, easy, and might be said to be brilliant except for one small detail.

Helen's fireplace is now tipped at a 30° angle.

KEEPING YOUR DRIVE ALIVE

#1: The first thing is to keep your goal visible. If you are trying to lose weight, put a picture of you at your fattest on the refrigerator door. If your goal is to be a successful apricot farmer, then subscribe to lots of apricot magazines.

#2: Write down your specific goals. Then post them where you will see them. They must be specific—so specific that anyone can tell whether you have achieved them. If you write, "I'm going to grow a lot of apricots," that is not specific. Instead, you might write, "I will have a thousand trees before my twenty-third birthday," or "I will be the largest apricot producer in Georgia by [put a specific date here]."

#3: In your reading of several hundred books, include biographies of people who have achieved great things. They don't all have to be stories of successful apricot growers. You'll find that one common theme will be their unstoppable determination. Their will was adamantine (= like a stone, imperturbable).

#4: Failure cannot kill your drive. Know that lots of setbacks are certain to be a part of your path to retiring in 24 years.

Michael Rubin wrote: *I was $120,000 in debt at 16. Rule number one is you can't be scared to fail.*

Question: Who is Michael Rubin?
Answer: His chosen field was online sports merchandise.
Question: Why should I listen to Michael Rubin?
Answer: At the age of 41, his net worth was $2,300,000,000. (That's $2.3 billion.)

Things are going to get rough. Your thousand apricot trees might develop some kind of apricot rot. Your central thought must be that if you are knocked down five times, you will get up six times.

Did you know that Walt Disney went broke seven times AND had a nervous breakdown before he and his pal Mickey Mouse succeeded?

#5: Which salesmen succeed? The ones that call on the most customers. And they are the ones who also have the greatest number of rejections. Talent takes second place to tenacity. Inner compulsion is it—have so much that it scares you. This will count much more than any inheritance.

#6: Your self-discipline—your drive—is directly related to where your eyes are looking. The further you look ahead, the easier it will be to wade through all the daily dreck.

#7: "They" are going to laugh at you. You are going to make unbelievably bad errors. Humiliation will try to knock the stuffing out of you *many times*. The cure? It's easy: Stop trying to think of yourself as King or Queen of the Universe. You are not the Big Cheese. You are just someone trying to do your work. High quality work does not mean error-free work.

If no one can find fault with you, something is really wrong!

Chapter Twenty-Two
The Big Picture

What good is happiness? It can't buy money.

—Henny Youngman

Fred was ready to reinvent himself. He would make founding a university a central focus of his life. Think. Dream. Plan. Set specific goals. Read many books. Accept setbacks.

At his own university he could also be a teacher. He wouldn't be limited to teaching from Monday to Friday. He could teach classes on Saturday if he wished.

He would hire a good president for his university—not someone who was continually off at conferences and vacations—someone who shared his vision of what it means to be truly well educated.

After a couple of years, his university would have at least a thousand students. If he set the annual tuition at $5,000 (which is "slightly" less than Stanford's $42,690), that would generate five million dollars each year (The math: $1,000 \times 5,000 = 5,000,000$).

He did the calculations for how many teachers he would need.[*] Forty teachers times an average salary of $60,000 equals $2,400,000.

Government-run universities love to have fancy buildings, football stadiums, parking garages, and big lawns. All this stuff is impressive, but the whole point of a university is to connect the students with what is best, truest, and most noble in our civilization. (Football ain't it.)

Fred had seen strip mall shopping centers where most of the stores are vacant. Many of the landlords would probably jump for joy if Fred's University offered to rent all their vacancies. Conversion to classrooms would be a cinch. And parking! No other university would have easy parking just steps away from the classroom.

---

[*] A thousand students will take 15 units per semester. Each teacher will teach 15 units per semester (which is the standard load for community colleges).

With an average of 25 in a class, the university would need 40 teachers. (The math: $25 \times 40 = 1,000$)

Fred had second thoughts about hiring a university president. What does a president really do? Instead, he would just need a bookkeeper to collect and deposit the thousand tuition checks and pay the bills and salaries.

Fred added up the expenses of salaries and rent and the miscellaneous items such as insurance. It all came to a little less than four million dollars.

Income = $5 million. Expenses = $4 million. Fred's eyes went ker-ching like a slot machine.

In less than a second he figured out that making a million dollars a year was more than the $600 per month he was now receiving from teaching at KITTENS.

The thought was almost intoxicating. He needed a little time to clear his head. He wandered down the hallway to one of the vending machines and bought a doughnut. He headed back to his office and put the doughnut in his desk "for later." He wasn't hungry right now. He had too much to think about.

Would having a lot of money be bad? he asked himself. He had paid attention in Sunday school and knew that money, itself, was not evil. He had heard the stories of good guys such as Abraham and Solomon who were blessed with tons of riches. It was all a matter of getting your priorities straight. It's the inordinate love of self that is the root of all evil. There are lots of bad things besides going crazy about money—such as a lust for power or insane jealousy. Hitler, Stalin, and Mao weren't looking to amass great wealth. Satan wasn't kicked out of heaven because he wanted to embezzle from God's checking account. Gold is so common there that they use it for paving streets.

Getting money is the perfect way to solve . . . money problems. But there are a lot of problems in life that a million dollars a year won't solve.

If you get great wealth, there is only one thing that is guaranteed: *You will have a lot of money.* Contentment isn't a part of that package.

Only the friends you had before you made the big bucks are the ones you can automatically trust. Do you remember the big parties in *The Great Gatsby*? Zillions of people, who couldn't care less about Mr. Gatsby, showed up to enjoy his lavish festivities .

Much of American society (What ever happened to *i before e, except after c*?) has gone nuts about money. It becomes *the* goal in life. People want to become doctors, dentists, lawyers, or bankers just so that they can make hundreds of thousands of dollars each year. Then everyone (they think) will look up to them. And what do they do with their $200,000/year income? They buy a million dollar house in a fancy neighborhood where all their neighbors have two million dollar houses. And they are the "poor folk" of the neighborhood. (What ever happened to *i before e, except after c*?)

Suppose one of your brothers decides that his calling is to make a lot of money. Suppose another one of your brothers wants to teach at a seminary. And another wants to be a manager at a fast food place so that he can have enough money to marry his sweetheart and rear a half dozen kids. Good luck and blessings on all of them! There is nothing *inherently* wrong with any of your brothers' ambitions.

The money-making brother might provide jobs for many people and might donate large amounts of money toward relieving people's suffering.

The brother who teaches at a seminary might inspire many future ministers to a deeper commitment.

The brother's wife and kids might be seven of the happiest people on earth. And he wouldn't trade any of his kids for a million dollars.

TWO IMPORTANT POINTS

Point #1: The goal in life is to collect **HAPPINESS POINTS**. It isn't to be famous, have a ton of money, or to have a big family—although these might be a source of **HAPPINESS POINTS** for some people.

Each of us have different ways of collecting **HAPPINESS POINTS**.

➤ Some might get lots of **HAPPINESS POINTS** from being strong and slender. Others might get an equal number of **HAPPINESS POINTS** from chocolate ice cream.

➤ Some would love to take vacations to exotic places six times a year. Others would hate to be sent to those hot, humid places.

➤ Some would get a big giggle in having a pet zebra in their backyard. For others, it would be a curse.

Point #2: It's not just **HaPPiNeSS PoiNtS** that we need to gather. We need **ReaL HaPPiNeSS PoiNtS**.

> *I, your reader, don't get it. Happy is happy, isn't it?*
> Not quite. **ReaL HaPPiNeSS PoiNtS** are those that last.

For example, you could get a temporary happy:
from drinking yourself into unconsciousness,
   from overdosing on banana creme pie,
     from killing the guy that really bugs you,
       from cheating to pass a test,
         from idleness,
           from lying to make a buck—
but none of these offer **ReaL HaPPiNeSS PoiNtS** because two weeks later they leave a bad taste in your mouth.

In contrast, you could get **ReaL HaPPiNeSS PoiNtS**:
from founding a university which offers a real education,
   from rearing clean cut kids,
     from donating blood every eight weeks,
       from doing your job well, even when the boss isn't looking,
         from being a Scout leader,
           from good eating and exercise.

ReaL HaPPiNeSS PoiNtS have two characteristics. First, they usually involve short-term pain now. Second, they switch from me-me-me-me-me to loving yourself *and* others.

Your contentment during the last third of your life will depend a lot on how many **ReaL HaPPiNeSS PoiNtS** you earned in the first two-thirds.

Chapter Twenty-three
Capital

They tickled. The ants were crawling up Fred's legs on their way to the doughnut that was in the desk drawer. He took the doughnut out of the drawer. The ants crawled across his chest and onto the arm that held the doughnut.

He tossed the doughnut into the waste basket. The ants retreated back across his chest and down his legs. They still tickled.

Fred dreamed about getting a desk with an ant-proof drawer so that he could safely store the food that he got "for later."

Life is full of distractions. Some are nice, and some are *ants*.

Fred was reading Prof. Eldwood's *Reasons Businesses Die*. It was one of the several hundred books that Fred was going to read in preparation for founding a university.

Eldwood wasn't a very good writer. He was hard to read. For example, *Reasons Businesses Die* begins:

> **Chief among the various impediments to longevity in businesses of all kinds is the propensity to lack sufficient capital—either through lack of foresight, or failure to do the requisite computations—in order to maintain a positive balance in a company's cash account during the initial years so that the cash flow and savings are not exhausted by startup and quotidian expenses.**

Fred made notes and summarized: Have enough money at the beginning to survive.

One of the biggest barriers to starting up a new business is the need for startup money. That is why many people begin their careers as employees.* The real danger of having a job is that you get too

---

* Acquiring enough startup capital is one reason to be employed at the beginning. The other reason is to get a job in your chosen field so that you can learn the business from the inside. Fred's teaching at KITTENS was an excellent way to learn many of the things he should and shouldn't do in running Fred's University.

comfortable. It's sometimes called hiding inside the womb of a corporation or of government. Being born—starting your own business—means breathing the air of freedom and new life. If babies were given the choice, many of them would elect never to be born—much to the distress of their mothers.

Many job holders never make the transition. They stay safe. They watch television after work rather than doing the preparation—the 5,000 hours. They hate to hear about others who have made the leap. They wishfully think that maybe later some opportunity will turn up. They are just like Fred buying a doughnut and putting it aside "for later."

If you want real wealth—the kind you can retire on—then you must take the plunge. You must risk.

And almost certainly, you will fail many times. That is just reality. The baseball players with the greatest home run records, such as Babe Ruth, also hold the record for the most strikeouts. When you are swinging for the fences, you leave the comfort zone of just trying to get on base.

Live long enough and you will hear plenty of stories of guys who were loyal "company men" who put in faithful service, year after year, and were "let go" at the age of 54. They are replaced either by cheaper younger employees or by automation.* Being loyal to a company does not mean that it will be loyal to you. And even if the owners of a company are totally committed to their employees, bankruptcies do happen. Do you want to have gray hair and be working at some minimum-wage job?

Fred was all fired up. He had moved from just dreaming into action. One of his tasks was to determine his startup capital needs. He had made a list of expenses he would face in founding Fred's University. He would have to rent some storefronts and remodel them. He would have business licenses and inspections. Advertising. Hiring teachers. A website. Office supplies.

---

* In a recent study, Carl Frey and Michael Osborne of Oxford University estimate that 47% of all U.S. jobs will be turned over to robots and computers in the next 20 years. Ouch!

Some of the things on this expenses list came from his years at KITTENS University. Many of them came from his reading.

He totaled his expenses list: $93,580. He could be certain that he hadn't thought of everything. Several books had told him: *There are always unexpected items.* Since being undercapitalized is one of the major reasons why new businesses fail, he adjusted the minimum capital he should raise to $120,000.

If Fred was going to fail, it was only going to be because of extremely bad luck—not for lack of diligence.

How to get the $120,000? Prof. Eldwood's *Money for Your New Business* listed seven ways: Win, Inherit, Marry, Steal, Partner, Earn, and Borrow. (Reading books is often a pleasant shortcut to having to figure everything out on your own. Fred was not the first one to need money. Many people might take hours to think of all seven ways that Eldwood listed in his book.)

Fred listed these seven ways on a piece of paper and wrote what he thought of each of them.

Win the Money

Some people spend their whole lives waiting to win the lottery. Rather than do the work of preparing to move from employed to employer, they buy some tickets and just hope. Instead of one chance in a zillion, I want my chances of achieving liberating wealth to be very high. I want to risk and sweat so that there is only a small chance I won't make it.

The chances of winning some big lottery are about the same as the chances of a duck with a necktie knocking on my office door and asking if I would like a ride on his airplane.

Inherit the Money

In some of Jane Austen's novels, this happens. But since I don't have any rich relatives, my chances are about zero.

Some people have rich uncles, but often their kids, not the nephews, get the inheritance.

Marry into Money

I'm six!

Steal

This is the way that C.C. Coalback likes to get money. Spending your "retirement" years in prison is only one drawback to this road to wealth.

There is a bigger drawback. Every person has a birthright to Life, Liberty, and Property. If you take away their life, you are a murderer. If you take away their liberty—kidnaping or slavery—you have taken away part of their life. That's another form of murder. If you take away someone's property, you take away what they have spent part of their life earning. They have exchanged part of their life and freedom* in order to own that car. If you take it, you take part of their life.

The biggest drawback to stealing/murder (life, liberty or property) is what it does to you.

small essay

What Hurting Others Does to You

Solipsism (SOL-ip-sism) is the belief that only you exist. The rest of the world is only an illusion–a show that is going on for your benefit. It's not that you are king or queen of the universe. It's worse. You *are* the universe. It is a really neat theory since it is really hard to disprove. But it is also very sick.

Every time you kill someone because they bug you (or steal from someone else) you become more solipsistic. Others don't really count.

There are many solipsists running around in our world. They are often sweet and charming on the outside. They do that to hide their belief so that they can get more for themselves. They are not the kind of people who live (or die) for others.

For Goodness' sake, don't marry a solipsist!

end of small essay

---

* Freedom? If you have a job and have to show up every weekday at 8 a.m., your body is probably not where it would like to be.

Chapter Twenty-four
Partnerships

Fred continued working on his list of ways to get the $120,000 to start his new business. He had already done Win, Inherit, Marry, and Steal. There were three left.

Get a Partner

Founding a university requires a lot of different skills and talents. I can supply my knowledge of teaching and of how a university should be set up. Someone else might have some business knowledge and know about payrolls, business law, and hiring. A third person might have $100,000 and could arrange to borrow the other $20,000.

What if we make a partnership? Each could contribute what they have. Each could promise to work as hard as possible. Each could get a third of the profits.

Fred talked with a bunch of really elderly people (more than 30 years old) who had been in partnerships. What he learned really surprised him.

Most of the time
Partnerships don't work.

Although they sound warm and friendly, although it feels good to think about my two friends and I working toward a common good, the reality is that a great number of partnerships end in fighting.

Even if your partners are your brother and your sister.

A partnership isn't a single entity (except legally speaking). It doesn't have a single mind. If Fred and two others form a partnership to found a university, there are three people involved—each with his/her own opinions. Fred would want an emphasis on English, math, science, history, etc.—the classical academic subjects. Another partner might insist that car repair and hotel management be included in the course offerings. The third might demand that all those majors that end in the word "Studies" be included.

Fred would want to keep expenses down by renting cheap strip mall vacancies. Another wants to build impressive buildings to highlight the grandeur of their university.

One says, "You gotta have a football team." Fred says, "You gotta be kidding."

Another difficulty with collective action is that there is a real incentive *not* to work hard. If the partnership has three people, any extra hour that I work will only put one-third of an hour's profit in my pocket. Any hour that I goof off instead of working takes only a third of an hour's profit out of my pocket.

When East and West Germany were split up after WWII, the only difference was the collectivist vs. free market economies they lived under. After the Berlin wall fell, the poverty vs. wealth between the two halves was very apparent. The same is true between North and South Korea.

A dog with three heads doesn't work. The solution? One head. It is Fred's university. He makes the decisions. Of course, he doesn't have all the skills and resources himself to make it all happen. He isn't going to build a computer or teach all the classes or have enough money in his savings.

He will buy (or rent) the computer.

He will hire teachers.

He will hire the money (known as borrowing).

If the teachers were partners with Fred instead of employees, they would have different objectives than just teaching well. If Fred hires someone to teach a course in differential equations for the fall semester, that teacher will concentrate on doing a good job so that he/she will be rehired for the spring.

Fred could contract for *any service* that he would need.

Chapter Twenty-five
Earn or Borrow

There were only two items left on Fred's list of ways to get startup capital for his business—earn it or borrow it. The other five ways (win, inherit, marry, steal, or partner) really don't work reliably.

Earn

Right now I make $600 per month. Even if I were to save it all, it would take 200 months to scrape up $120,000.

$$600\overline{)120000}^{200}$$

Of course, when I'm ten years old, I'll be making $1,000 per month, but still that's going to be almost forever before I can open the doors for my university.

Borrow

I read in Prof. Eldwood's *The Complete Guide to Debtors' Prisons* that there are two kinds of debt: good debt and bad debt. He wrote that good debt is borrowing in order to make money. Borrowing to start a business is one of the best debts—assuming that you have done the 5,000 hours of preparation.

Fred thought about how Helen was borrowing in order to get a sofa and a fireplace. He had heard that she was going to take a two-week vacation to Hawaii before she started teaching in the fall. Her credit cards would all be maxed out before classes started. Bad debt.

Fred had two obvious difficulties. First, was his extremely low salary. Any teacher with five years of very successful teaching should be able to find a teaching position that paid much more than his current $7,200 per year. Teachers of math and science are usually in much more demand than those who teach sociology or Italian literature.

Fred's second difficulty is that founding a university takes a lot more startup capital than, say, starting a home alarm system company. In the book *Super Cool Businesses* Fred had seen a chapter on how to start a business that specialized in home alarms. It had talked about burglar

alarms and fire alarms and specialty alarms such as pendant alarms that
old people could wear. If they fell down and couldn't get up, they could
just press the alarm that they were wearing. There were kid alarms so that
if a kid was home alone and cut himself, he could signal for help. That
apocryphal book was written in 1990 and seemed a bit out of date.
Nowadays, old folks and kids can easily carry cells phones in their
pockets. But cell phones aren't smart enough (yet) to detect a burglary in
progress when the owners are away.

Fred thought to himself Life is often so messy. First, I need my
teaching job at KITTENS in order to get some startup capital and learn about how a
university works. Then I might have to start with an alarm system business
because I can't earn or borrow enough money to found a university. The years are
slipping by! Next year I'm going to be 7.
   No bank is going to lend me $120,000. Some banks won't even lend a
nickel to a six-year-old.

Moments of despair are very common on the road to significant
wealth. If Fred were to just continue teaching at KITTENS University
until the age of 65, things for him would be a lot simpler.
   Most people take the simpler, easier way. That's why they are
called the 99%. Many have money problems in the last twenty years of
their lives and wish that they had done things differently.

If starting an alarm company is what I have to do Fred thought, then that
is what I'll do. My real goal—where my heart lies—is in education. I am a teacher.
Founding a university is the game I want to play.

So Fred sat down and opened *Wiring Home Alarm Systems.*

This was all new to Fred. The only
thing he understood in the diagram was the
burglar and the flower pot.
   Learning new stuff can take time, effort,
pain, concentration, and sacrifice. Knowing
what his ultimate goal was gave Fred an iron will.

Basic alarm diagram

Chapter Twenty-six
Failure

I am defeated all the time;
yet to victory I am born.

—Emerson

Fred didn't have any rich relatives. None of his students had any significant amounts of money. Right now, the only path to capital was Fred's Alarm and Safety Company. (He thought that sounded better than just Fred's Alarm Company.)

After reading several wiring books he learned the difference between a capacitor and a resistor. After ten hours of reading it all started to make sense.

52 Common Symbols

Fred found a basic alarm kit on the Internet and located a student who knew how to install it.

The only thing left was the selling. At first, he was thinking of going door-to-door and doing the selling himself. He realized that there was a better way. He knew many students who would be happy to pick up some extra money. He located a dozen of them and would pay them on commission. (They would get 10% of each alarm system they sold.)

He bought 50 of the alarm kits (so that he could get a wholesale discount). He bought advertising on the radio and in the newspaper. He paid $120 to the local government for the piece of paper called a business license. In all, he spent all his cash, $5,630. That left $13 in his KITTENS pension fund. He was broke.

None of the kits sold. Each was designed to only protect one window or door. If someone opened the window, it would make a buzzing sound. No homeowner thought that would be very effective. Fred hadn't researched the kits before he bought them. He had relied on the pretty pictures on the kit's website of burglars being caught and sent to prison.

The dozen student salesmen all quit.

Fred ~~had failed~~. No. His business had failed. He had read many biographies of men and women who had accomplished great things in their lives. Every one of the them had had many painful setbacks in their lives. None of their lives had been a bed of roses—unless you think of trying to take a nap lying on a thorny rose bush.

Fred's Alarm and Safety Company was supposed to be his stepping stone from teaching at KITTENS to founding a university. Instead of a stepping stone, it was more like a deep hole he had stepped into. He was worse off than before he had begun that company.

Back in Chapter 1, we mentioned that Kingie had built a fort in the corner of the office so that he could protect himself from Fred's pet cat.

Fred now offered the 50 unsold alarm kits to Kingie. Kingie was reluctant to take them because his fort had more than a hundred doors and windows.

Since Kingie was always in the office, no burglar was going to break into his fort without his noticing. Even for free, those kits weren't worth much at all.

Fred had to try something else. For about a week, he investigated starting Fred's Lawn Care. He offered to cut lawns for $5. The kids in the neighborhood would cut them for $3. ~~Fred's Lawn Care~~.

Fred's Surf Boards. No oceans in Kansas.
Fred's KITTENS Tours. You don't need a guide to see the rose gardens.
Fred's Party Planning. There were few parties in August.
Fred's Pagers. Everyone has a cell phone.
Fred's Travel Agency. Everyone uses the Internet to plan their trips.

You gotta say this for Fred. He's tough. He gets knocked down and he pops up again, like one of those inflatable clowns that you can punch and it comes right back up again.

Summer was almost gone. Tomorrow would be the first day of classes at KITTENS. Helen was back from Hawaii. Her office had been outfitted with the newest hexaphonic double-deloopy sound and lights system. For an extra $2,300 she got the planetarium add-on package that could project on her office ceiling the star configuration for any night in the last thousand years. She thought she needed that in case some student asked what the night sky looked like when Christina Rosetti was composing *Twilight Calm*, which contains the lines:

> *In separate herds the deer*
> *Lie; here the bucks, and here*
> *The does, and by its mother sleeps the fawn:*
> *Through all the hours of the night until the dawn*
> *They sleep, forgetting fear.*

Wait! Stop! Enough! I, your reader, need to ask a big question. Back in Chapter 10 you were talking about investing in the Five Asset Classes and using fancy logarithms to show that retirement could be 24 years away.

That wasn't *fancy* logs. I was only solving exponential equations using the Birdie rule, which every second-year algebra student can do.

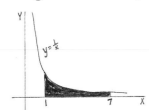

Fancy logs are used in second semester calculus where we show that the area under the curve $y = \dfrac{1}{x}$ from x = 1 to x = 7 is exactly equal to ln 7, where ln 7 is the natural log of 7, which is $\log_{2.7182818284590452353602874713527} 7$.

Logs, schmogs! I'm interested in that 24 years. Fred has gone bust in seven different businesses (alarms, lawn care, surf boards, tours, party planning, pagers, and a travel agency). Time's a-wasting. Are you going back on your prediction?

Heavens no. Twenty-four years is my best estimate for individuals who do the preparation (5,000 hours), who take the required action and who are willing to experience big-time failure. It's been a month since Fred began. In that month Fred has been tossed on his back seven times. He is broke.

Of course, that means that he's a month behind.

No! He's a month into those 24 years. In the calculations in Chapter 10, I assumed a growth rate of 6% per year. That might be true for paper assets, but that isn't true when you finally start a business that succeeds.

Let's suppose you finally start that successful business in the 19th year of your 24-year quest. You'll notice that I'm being very conservative. I didn't say in the 8th year of your quest. I'm allowing plenty of time for preparation and failures.

In that 19th year (which is year one of the business) you have 5,000 hours of reading and other preparation behind you. You are now well acquainted with failure. You have learned (painfully) what not to do. If the business is founding a university, you might only have 40 students, have hired two teachers and rented one strip mall store space. And it might feel like another failure is coming.

In year two, those students tell their friends about the wonderful education they are getting. Ninety students enroll for the fall semester.

Year three brings writeups in several magazines and several requests for radio interviews. And 370 students.

Year four is the year that a thousand students enroll. Do you remember what that meant? Four chapters ago, we computed that at this point Fred's net income would cross $1,000,000 per year.

By year five, you have 10,000 hours of study and experience in your chosen business.

What might surprise you, is that at this point there will be only one or two hundred people *in the world* who are your peers in your field.

Unless you have lost your liberty (prison) or your health, you will be as rich as Kingie with his 17 safes in his fort all stuffed with cash.

T here were many unknowns in the path that lay ahead for Fred. He could not predict the future—but he could strongly influence it. The only handle by which he could seize the future was the handle called **now**.

But right now his age was a bit of a handicap. In about 12 years, he will be able to legally sign contracts (get credit cards, buy real estate, hire workers). This was a handicap that he would outgrow.

It's the opposite handicap—being a senior citizen with little income and preparation—that is really tough to overcome.*

Fred thought about his height. He had been 36 inches tall for several years now. That might be a difficulty if he wanted to become a bull fighter or a policeman. But founding a university doesn't require being tall.

He had read the biographies of many great people. A bunch of them had been imprisoned. (If you can't name at least three, you haven't read enough biographies.) Fred asked himself What if I have to spend time in prison? He knew the answer: I have hundreds of books that I need to read there in order to prepare to found a university.

---

* Some people think of Colonel Sanders and his Kentucky Fried Chicken as an example of economic success later in life.

When he was about 30 years old, he established a ferry boat company. It was a big success. He sold the company for a lot of money and established a company that made acetylene lamps. That company failed when electric lamps became popular.

When he was about 40, he lived and worked at a service station and started cooking chicken, ham, and steaks for the customers. He served them in his service station living quarters. (You can't do that nowadays.)

After another ten years he had put the final touches on creating his "Secret Recipe" for cooking chicken in a pressure fryer.

Finally, when he was 65, he traveled around the United States and sold franchise rights to people to open KFC restaurants. When he was about 74, he sold the Kentucky Fried Chicken corporation for $2 million.

Fred wondered if there were any other obstacles that lay in his path to wealth. Dying was the first thing that came to mind. It's not just grandfathers and grandmothers who die. Pedestrians get hit by cars. Wars kill civilians of all ages. Bullets fly around in many inner cities.

Fred giggled. He wasn't worried about the afterlife. He knew what lies ahead after he dies. He giggled thinking about what the obituary in *KITTEN Caboodle* newspaper might read: FRED DIES IN MIDLIFE. That would be so silly.

He thought about ill health as a barrier to founding a university. Again, there are no guarantees that he will be able to achieve any goal, but he knew that good health habits increase his odds of success.

✓ He exercises. His jogging is legendary. He works out in his office using books as dumbbells.

✓ He doesn't smoke or drink.

✓ He isn't fat.

✓ He doesn't worry and fret. That can take years off your life.

✓ He flosses and brushes his teeth and sees the dentist regularly.

His eating habits however need a lot of improvement. Drinking sugary Sluice and skipping many meals—it's no surprise that at six years old he is only three feet tall.

Fred had read a biography of Colonel Sanders. When the Colonel was about 19 years old, he married Josephine King. When he was on a business trip, his boss fired him. Before he could get back home, Josephine gave away all their furniture and left him. Josephine's brother sent Sanders a letter: "She had no business marrying a no-good fellow like you who can't hold a job."

Fred knew that one very important key in founding a university (or any other major life goal) is to have a supportive spouse. Choosing the right one is one of the two or three most important decisions of life.

Fred wasn't quite ready to do the "marriage thing" yet. That was good. Marriages begun when the partners are younger than 18 have about twice the divorce rate of those where the partners are older than 25.

Some people spend more time choosing a car than in finding a spouse. Most Americans seem to just pick someone that they happen to meet—in a class, down the street, or at a party. Is it surprising that we have such a high divorce rate?

The alternative is to make a deliberate and intelligent effort to find the one who will be right for you.

At the church I was at about 30 years ago, the minister told us how he did pre-marital counseling. One of the first questions he would ask the couple is, "Why do you want to get married?" If the only answer was, "We're in love," he would shock them by announcing that he didn't want to perform the marriage ceremony.

He explained in his sermon that I heard that being in love is a very temporary state. Nature uses "being in love" to connect people together initially. They stare into each other's eyes. They sit on a blanket in the woods. Some even write songs or poems.

But, after a year or two, the "bloom is off the rose." (That's the expression he used.) No one is playing the game of being on their best behavior anymore. You have seen them when they are grouchy or angry. You know their bathroom habits. You have found the things that drive your partner crazy. You have found the things your partner does that drive you nuts.

How do you make that deliberate and intelligent effort to find that supportive spouse? Here are some suggestions:

#1: The encounters with the opposite sex during teenage and early twenties are often filled with shyness. When I, your author, was a senior in college, I took a statistics class. Across the room was a girl I found very attractive. She was outgoing and talked with the students around her. I never sat closer to her. I knew her full name. I never said a word to her during the whole semester. At the library I saw a book: *Overcoming Shyness*, but was too embarrassed to pull it off the shelf.

Overcoming shyness is a skill that can be learned—no, it *must* be learned. Unless you plan on living like a hermit alone out on your farm, becoming competent in meeting people is essential in ① owning any business and ② dating.

#2: To find a good life-long partner, *after* you have become a competent dater, you will date dozens of possible candidates. Those that you date before that time won't be seeing the real you—only the tongue-tangled kid. Meeting dozens means that you are not marrying the second one you date.

#3: Make lunch dates, not dinner dates, for that initial meeting. There is no giant rush to intimacy. You are meeting in public, not at either one's house or apartment. Just to get to know them a little. If he/she eats the mashed potatoes with his/her hands, that might be enough to let you be glad you didn't elect to spend two hours on a dinner date.

#4: Learn how to end a relationship. Without that skill, you are committed to marriage after you have dated three times. Sometimes, all it takes to end things is not phoning.

If you don't know how to break up, then you certainly can't be at ease in meeting others. It places a TREMENDOUS BURDEN on you if you have to decide whether you are going to marry someone before agreeing to the third date.

If you are dating someone who is not a competent dater, perhaps the worst way to dial down a relationship is to write a letter, especially a big long one detailing exactly why thcy failed as a potential partner. Breaking up is hard enough without adding to their pain.

#5: After you have dated dozens and are at the point of thinking "this one might be it," two steps are important before you move on to being engaged. It's much easier to break up with someone you are going steady with than with someone you are engaged to. **One step** is spending a lot of time in a lot of different circumstances with him/her. See how they spend their money. Learn about any alcohol, drug, or anger problems they have. See if they treat cashiers and waiters like human beings or like scum. Meet the potential in-laws. Some in-laws can make a virtual hell out of your marriage. **The other step** is to spend a lot of time talking about the important things (other than just how lovely their eyes are). Talk about life goals, about religion, about the number of children you want, about finances.

One important financial choice is whether you want to keep your money separate from theirs. If you keep it separate, then you will not have to be disturbed by the foolish (in your eyes) ways they spend their dollars. Too many marriages are ruined by fighting over a jointly held money.

All of these suggestions are hard work. Do them only if you want to be happy.

Chapter Twenty-eight
Brain Games

The human brain is the most complicated thing in the universe. Understanding algebra or chemistry is much easier than figuring out that three-pound mass of jellied pudding that sits between your ears.

Most newborn babies are a body with a brain attached. Fred was a brain with an attached body. He used his body to carry around his brain.

When he was a day or two old, he was trying to explain to his mother what a function is.[*] Yet, with all that brain power, he could never understand why he failed to do things he knew he should do and did things that he shouldn't.

> *It just might be*
> *impossible for a brain*
> *to understand itself.*   I'm not sure.

Fred heard many stories from English and history teachers who would assign 15-page papers. They told Fred tales of students who would stay up all night writing their papers at the very last moment.

☛ The students knew months ahead when the paper was due.

☛ Staying up all night was painful, but many of them habitually wrote their papers this way.

☛ These last-minute papers were usually horrible messes.

. . . and yet they did it. Were those students hoping to die before the paper was due? Were they hoping the teacher would change the due date or cancel the paper?

---

[*] You start with two sets, A and B. A function is any rule which assigns to each element of A exactly one element of B.

If A is the set of nickels in my pockets and B is the set of numbers, one possible function assigns each nickel to the year stamped on the coin.

Another possible function assigns nickels in my left pocket to 398 and nickels in my right pocket to 935,001,218.

Some people put off going to the dentist for years until their teeth hurt so bad that they can't stand it. It would have been much more pleasant to have that little cavity filled a couple of years earlier.

Ninety-nine percent practice putting off things.

Putting off having kids until you are 55 has some real drawbacks.

Excuses, excuses.

Question: Suppose you plan on dying five years from now. Wouldn't that be a great excuse for not beginning the 24 years to retirement?

Answer: Hardly! If you were to start that planting in a circle

and only did five year's worth and passed that along to your child, that would mean that you would be making your child's retirement come five years earlier—a gift of five years. What a gift!

Procrastination is only one of the games that your mind likes to play. There are many others.

There is the **STAYING HEALTHY GAME**. Suppose there are two weeks

till your hundredth birthday. A big celebration is planned. There is a major connection between mind and body. Your mind tells your body to stay alive for those two weeks. Many more people die in the two weeks after their big party than in the two weeks beforehand.

Lots are sick in bed on the day of a final exam that they dread. Few are sick on the days they are starring in a school play.

There is the **WINDFALL GAME**. You are in the attic going through a bunch of stuff that your aunt left when she died several years ago. You find $540 in one of her old purses. You call up your friends and take them all out to a fancy dinner. You buy the whole collection of music CDs of your favorite singing cowboy. It is found money, a windfall.

Party time!

Instead, you get your monthly check. With the recent raise, it's now $540 more than it used to be. It's *earned money*, not *found money*. You save/invest it.

This is a brain game. In reality, that $540 is $540 regardless of how you received it. It *should* all go into the pot marked income, but that is not how many people operate. People who win a $100,000 lottery—money they haven't spent years working hard to accumulate—go on spending sprees. It doesn't take long for them to be back at the place they were before they got the windfall.

There is the **FALLING IN LOVE GAME**. You see him/her across a crowded room. It's love at first sight. Your brain automatically fills in every good trait for that person.

They have no body odor. They sing on key. They don't have a big ugly tattoo on their back. They aren't married.

Your brain never seems to fill in the unseen details with just average qualities. Hemorrhoids and haphephobia (abnormal fear of being touched) never enter your mind.

There is the ⌊I⌋T'S ⌊F⌋REE ⌊G⌋AME. Our brains are hardwired to respond irrationally to anything that's marked FREE! We almost can't help ourselves.

If chocolate cakes are on sale for 10¢, we'll buy a dozen of them. If they are marked FREE! we'll fill up our car trunk with them.

Have you ever been to conferences or home shows that offer free key rings, pencils, and refrigerator magnets? You fill up your shopping bag with them (and throw them away when you get home). But if they cost a penny each, you wouldn't touch them.

The Price of Fred Books

For years several of my friends have told me I should increase the prices of the *Life of Fred* books. They pointed out that my *Life of Fred: Calculus Expanded Edition* book, which covers all two years of college calculus, is only $49. There is nothing comparable in the market for under $150.

I told them that I wanted to keep the prices really cheap. I wasn't writing to make a buck.

They smiled and said, "Okay. Double the prices and offer: BUY ONE AND GET ONE FREE! People will love it. Lots of stores do that."

I don't want to do that.

Chapter Twenty-nine
A Checklist

Kingie got interrupted again. A couple of times a day the armored truck would roll up to the Math Building. An armed guard would climb the stairs and present Kingie with another suitcase of money from his painting sales. Kingie would stop painting and wipe his hands. He would take the suitcase into his fort and drag it up to the third floor where his 17 safes are. When you are only six inches tall, you drag a suitcase, not carry it.

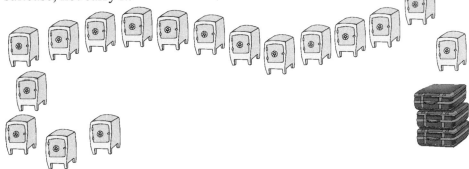

The safes were completely full, so Kingie just stacked the suitcases against a wall. He pulled a couple hundred dollar bills out of a suitcase so that he could buy more painting supplies.

Then he could get back to his passion, which was oil painting. The wealth came as a byproduct. When you are one of the best one or two hundred in the world—in almost any field—money will come almost automatically.

Fred was one month into his quest to found a university. Of the seven ways to get startup capital (win, inherit, marry, steal, partner, earn, and borrow), he knew that only earning and borrowing were reasonable. He needed $120,000.

In this month he had tried seven different businesses that required very little capital to start. None of them had worked. Tomorrow classes would start. Teaching would take a "small" chunk out of his day (8 till 5 with a five-minute break at 3). He knew that he would keep reading books about founding a university and would try other low-capital-to-start businesses.

No bank would lend to him. None of his students had $120,000. He knew that he would have to earn the startup capital since he couldn't find a lender.

It would be another three or four months before the obvious source of funding would dawn on Fred. (In case you need a hint, please reread the first two paragraphs of this chapter.)

Classes for the fall semester this year started on Wednesday. Today, Tuesday, students and faculty were settling in. Many of them had spent the summer in idleness. Fred often wondered how the students would do if they had to retake today the final exams they took at the end of the previous spring semester.*

Helen was busy meeting other faculty members and showing off her Hawaiian tan. She invited them to come see how she had decorated her office. Out of curiosity many of them came and looked and left. They were unimpressed by her extravagance and thought that she was just a rich young kid trying to show off, knowing that no teacher could afford new furniture and a fireplace on the salary that KITTENS paid.

Fred was trying to get as much reading done as he could on this last day before classes. He was deep into Prof. Eldwood's *Checklist of Personal Habits for Success.* He had just finished the chapter entitled "Don't Show Off." Eldwood wrote that most kids learn by the time that they are teenagers that showing off and bragging does not win friends. It breeds envy. Others will feel resentment when you talk about having stuff that they can't have.

If you invited Kingie out to lunch, he would talk about a thousand aspects of painting: great artists, new oil painting techniques, abstract art vs. photo-realism, and so on. He would never mention all the money that was piling up in his fort.

The rule is simple: *If you're a success, zip the lip.*

---

* The studies have been done. Most students would flunk the exam.

I, your reader, have a small question. Does that mean that I'm only supposed to talk about my failures?

Prof. Eldwood also writes about that in his "Don't Show Off" chapter. He asks you to think about what your reaction would be if someone tells you:

> My cat died last week. My car is turning into a cash
> eater. Last week I had to spend $2,300 on a front end
> alignment and now the brakes are going. My landlord
> won't replace my old refrigerator. I lost my job
> yesterday because my boss didn't like my attitude.
> My stomach has been real sour lately. I hope it isn't
> cancer. I'm terrified of what next month is going to
> bring.

Other than a little schadenfreude (SHAH-den-froi-deh), you wouldn't want to listen to much of that failure talk either.

But this doesn't make sense. I need to know. If I can't talk about my super successes and I can't talk about my misfortunes, what's left?

My, me, I, mine, my, I, my—do you see a little pattern there? It might be that only your mother (when she's not too busy) wants to hear about you.

On the first date you don't brag about yourself and don't bemoan your many shortcomings. They want to know who you are. They want to know if they want to go on a **second date** with you. Talk a bit

about what interests you. What your major was in college. Who you admire. Your hobbies. But keep it short. If your hobby is making popcorn, don't spend a half hour talking about the four different methods of popping the corn and fifteen different recipes for caramelizing it. If you bore the socks off of him/her on the first date, he/she surely won't want to spend the rest of their lives with you (and your popcorn).

On about the **third date**, it's appropriate to disclose that you are an alcoholic, that early onset dementia runs in your family, etc. Keeping those things secret until you are engaged is really unfair to the other person.

Prof. Eldwood's *Checklist of Personal Habits for Success* had a chapter on "Your Appearance." He said that much depends on what kind of business you are in.

If you are out drilling oil wells in Oklahoma, you will need different clothes than if you are running a candy store in Detroit. If you are in an office, dress a little bit better than your fellow employees but don't dress up so much that you make your boss look like a bum. If you are working at home as a computer programmer or a writer or an artist, you can go naked as long as you don't frighten your cat to death.

If you are a man teaching at a high school or college and some of the others wear a coat and tie, then you do too. And wear shoes that can be shined—and shine them. The instructions are on the shoe polish can.

For women, the general guidelines are to avoid too much jewelry, too much perfume, and too much makeup. Imitate your boss's boss.

And go easy on the false eyelashes.

Prof. Eldwood's *Checklist of Personal Habits for Success* listed three keys to success in the chapter "Talking, Looking & Shaking."

When you answer the phone, sound friendly. Don't make it sound like they have called a mortuary. (Of course, if you do work in a funeral home. . . .) The phone should never ring more than twice. You want to limit their frustration. You are not a government agency. (Of course, if you are a government agency. . . .)

Think of yourself as the customer. Do you really *enjoy* getting one of those phone machines that says: You have reached the XYZ company. For Spanish press 3, for English press 4. Our menu has recently changed. Listen carefully and select one of these options. For help in installing our FQ87 model, press 1. For regional matters, press 2. For questions about our model Z727, press 3. For inter-local assistance press 4. For international orders, press 5. For warranty matters visit our website at http: www/XYZ_Company/external_relations/first_six_days.com. To repeat this menu press *. I'm sorry. Due to unexpectedly high volume, response to your call might be delayed.

Your patience is appreciated. Here is some yodeling cowboy music to keep you entertained until we find someone to answer your call.

In the "looking" part of the chapter, Eldwood talks about eye contact. You are not a bowed slave whose eyes are on the ground. Nor are you some cow that is looking out the window for entertainment. Look 'em in the eye without staring. Make them feel they have your total attention—even if you're only making $8 an hour.

Whether you are an employee or an employer, you want to project energy. When you walk . . .

> head erect—not down
>> back straight—not slumped
>>> hands in natural motion—not in your pockets
>>> walking briskly—you are on the move.

In the "shaking" part of the chapter, Eldwood teaches how to shake hands. If you are a clerk at Harry's Hardware, you won't be shaking hands with customers. But there are situations where a handshake is appropriate.

Don't offer just fingers . . . unless you are expecting them to kiss your hand.

Don't offer them a dead fish handshake. Pretend like you are still alive.

Don't crush their hands with an ultra macho squeeze. Politicians who have to shake a hundred hands (pretending that they care about each and every voter) dread the idiot who wants to crush their hand into spaghetti.

Prof. Eldwood's *Checklist of Personal Habits for Success* most important chapter was entitled "Reputation." How you treat your customers does make a big difference. Customers do talk to others.

If you make promises, keep them. This, in itself, will differentiate your business from many others. If you say you are going to do something, then do it—even if it's inconvenient. Who wants to do business with a liar?

Don't be late. Being on time announces that you care about them and that you are not pretending to be King/Queen of the Universe.

Exceed what is expected. You are going to give them *more* and you are going to deliver *early*.

Your reputation is valuable. In fact, it's invaluable.

Prof. Eldwood's *Checklist of Personal Habits for Success* has a chapter on "Learning to Negotiate."

We are negotiating all the time. Two young brothers are arguing who gets to sit in the good chair when they watch television. Or three heirs are trying to decide how to split up the household goods that were left to them. Or two people are talking about getting married. (Yes. That involves give-and-take. She might ask for a well-kissed cheek and a restaurant dinner every week.)

Having skills in negotiating can mean hundreds of dollars when you buy a car. It can mean thousands of dollars when you buy or sell a house.

When you are a little kid, you have few negotiating skills. You say to your sister, "Do that or I will hit you." (Some countries operate on that level.)

When you are a little older, you learn a bit more. You say to your sister, "If you do that for me, I'll give you my Halloween candy." (This doesn't work very well in April.)

In the adult world, there are many key points to learn in making a deal more successful for you.

For example, always prepare in advance as much as possible. If you are going to buy a car, research on the Internet and talk with friends. Know what you want in a car. Know the prices.

For example, the one who is willing to walk away is almost always the one who gets the most in a deal. If the car you are most interested in is on three different car lots, talk with the sales person on the first lot. Learn everything they are willing to tell you. Enter into talk about the price. Then leave just when things are getting "serious." Tell them you need time to consider their offer. Stand up, thank them, and head out the door. It will be tough to do. When you get to the second car lot, you will know a lot more about the real bottom price for that car. If necessary, you can always go back to the first car lot (even though they have told you lies such as "This price is only good right now" or "We might sell the car to someone else if you don't buy it right now.")

For example, price is only one of the things you include in a negotiation. The other terms of the deal are often just as important.

At the very minimum, read three books on learning how to negotiate. It will be time well spent. There is much to learn.

Chapter Thirty
Insurance

F red had just finished reading the last pages of Prof. Eldwood's *Checklist of Personal Habits for Success* when he heard a knock on his office door. He knew that it wasn't the armed guard delivering another suitcase of money to Kingie, because he had just had a delivery. Fred was wrong. The guard had a second suitcase for Kingie. He had missed it in the armored truck when he had taken in the first suitcase. Normally, people don't get two suitcases of money on the same delivery.

As the guard was leaving, a man in a suit walked up to Fred and said, "Are you Fred Gauss?" Fred nodded.

"I'm your insurance agent."

Fred was confused. "I don't have an insurance agent."

"Yes you do. My company has assigned me to all the faculty on this campus."

This was, perhaps, not the best way to start a relationship. Most people like to think that they choose their agent, not get chosen by their agent.

He continued, "May I have a few moments of your time to explain to you all the insurance policies that you need?" He walked into Fred's office, sat down at Fred's desk, and opened his briefcase.

Fred went into deep think. It was a big question.

small essay
Who Owns You?

When you are a kid, your parents can decide when you need to turn out your lights and go to bed, what toothpaste you will use, and, in some cases, whether you should be put to death. (Deuteronomy 21:18-21)

As an adult, the situation is a little different. The government will tell you which light bulbs you can use (no incandescents), which plants you can smoke, and whether you will face almost certain death in a military situation. (Many people have a longer life expectancy on death row than in a gun fight in some far off country in an undeclared war.)

There are four basic kinds of government, and they all **are defined in terms of ownership.** Very briefly, they are . . .

Socialist: Government owns the businesses.

Communist: Government owns everything: the businesses, your cars, your house.

Fascist: Government claims that you own your stuff, but issues so many regulations and laws that, in effect, they are running things. The nation is the supreme controlling boss in everyone's life.

Freedom (the free market): You own your own stuff. You can sell it or trade it or use it to make money. You can make as much money as you like and no one, including government, can take it from you. The only job that government has is to protect you from the force or fraud (lying) of others. You can do anything as long as you don't instigate aggression against others.

Everyone who wants to control other peoples' property wants socialism, communism, or fascism. Other people produce, and you use the government to "legally" take it from them. That's called being a parasite.

Everyone who is productive considers life and property to be their inalienable right. If they elect to give to others, it is true charity because it is voluntary.

end of small essay

So Fred said to the insurance salesman, "I choose to *give* you 15 minutes of my time." This wasn't charity. Fred didn't know much about insurance. This would be a good way to learn.

The insurance man began, "First, let's start with auto insurance. As you know, the government requires each car owner to carry some insurance." Fred mentally translated this: The government is forcing me to buy something whether I want to or not. Fascism?

Fred said, "I don't own a car."

"What about life insurance? Everyone should have some."

Fred asked, "Why?"

"So that if you die, your relatives can get a bunch of money."

Fred tried to think of who his needy relatives were. Kingie surely didn't need an extra suitcase full of money. Fred shook his head.

"What about homeowner's insurance? Do you own a home?"

Fred shook his head again.

"Then you must need renter's insurance to protect all the things that you own."

Fred looked around his office. He had a lot of books, his jogging clothes, and the food in his desk. The books were worth about $500. His jogging clothes were almost rags; he had jogged many miles in them. The food in his desk was covered with ants.

The agent took out a big poster.

The agent said, "Only $3 for every thousand dollars of protection."

Fred had several questions. "Isn't a tsunami a giant sea wave? Aren't we in Kansas—a thousand miles from the ocean? Aren't big earthquakes mostly on the West Coast?"

"You gotta admit," the agent said, "our rates are really low."

"Penguin attack? Are they going to migrate all the way from the south pole and climb the two flights of the Math Building and eat my books? How about insurance from fire and tornado damage?"

The agent grinned. "Those are special add-ons and cost a lot more." Quickly, he changed the subject and said, "Getting insurance is something that every responsible person needs to do."

Fred played with that sentence in his head: That means that if I'm responsible, then I should get insurance. That means that if I don't buy insurance, then I'm not a responsible person. That feels like a lie.

Fred said, "Well, your 15 minutes are up. Goodbye." The agent left after putting his business card on Fred's desk.

In terms of good financial choices, insurance can be a good thing if you buy it wisely.

The reason for insurance is
to protect you
from financial catastrophe.

A single dad with three young kids probably needs life insurance until he has created a good fortune (as Jane Austen called it). His death would be a financial catastrophe. On the other hand, the death of any of his kids would not have a large financial impact.

If you have a decent amount of assets, then insurance to protect against lawsuits (valid *or* frivolous) is necessary in American society. Part of auto insurance, for example, provides some lawsuit protection.

When you buy a gadget in a store and they offer an extended warranty, you should decline it. They are offering insurance for something that would not be a financial catastrophe.

An **insurance deductible** is the amount you pay before the insurance company pays. With a $4,000 loss, a $500 deductible means that you would receive $3,500 from the company. Higher deductibles means lower rates. Choose the highest deductible that wouldn't be a financial catastrophe for you to pay.

It's been a while since we've had a *Your Turn to Play*. Please get out a piece of paper and write your answers before you peek at my answers on the next page. Please.

Your Turn to Play

1. There are psychological barriers to getting/keeping a good fortune. If you have been told all your life that the best that you can hope for is being a store cashier or a secretary, what should you do?

2. Which of these offers the most **HaPPiNeSS PoiNtS**?

   A) Gaining a million dollars and having your net worth go from $49 million to $50 million.

   B) Gaining an extra $800 and being able to now pay the rent.

3. Which of these is important in earning a good fortune?

   A) Feeling/knowing that there is nothing wrong with having lots of money.

   B) Having sufficient startup capital before starting your chosen business.

   C) Being willing to take appropriate risks.

   D) Knowing that money is not just going to fall in your lap without serious effort.

   E) Being willing to make that effort.

   F) All of the above.

4. Your insurance agent offers an add-on to your auto policy. For a little extra cost you can get towing if your car is disabled. Yes or no?

5. You are offered hospital insurance. If you are hospitalized, the company pays the bills. Yes or no?

6. (Hard question) You buy auto insurance for your new $50,000 car that will pay you if your car is damaged in a collision. Suppose you have the choice between a $200 deductible and a $1,000 deductible.

   You choose the $1,000 deductible because your rates will be cheaper, and this is the largest available deductible you can afford.

   There is another reason to choose the $1,000 deductible. Name it.

·······COMPLETE SOLUTIONS·······

1. That's easy. Don't believe them.

There are zillions of people who have risen from trailer park to mansion. Many of the super rich have earned their fortunes rather than have inherited them. Read their biographies as an antidote to the poison of, "You can't make anything of yourself."

2. B) Gaining the $800.

In mathematics we say that **HaPPiNeSS PoiNtS** are not a linear function of dollars received. If you double your income, you do not automatically double your happiness.

Going from $49 million to $50 million probably won't change what you eat, what you wear, or where you live.

3. F)

4. No. Don't insure for things that you can handle yourself. Paying the cost of a tow won't put you into poverty.

5. Yes. Stays in the hospital often cost thousands of dollars a day. Three days in the hospital and the bill might be $21,931.07—this is not unusual. Many bankruptcies are because of medical expenses.

Here it is important to shop around and compare what different insurance companies offer. The terms and prices will vary.

6. Suppose your car door is slightly dented. The repair would be $300.

If you have a $1,000 deductible, the insurance company will not owe you anything. You just go and get it fixed and pay the $300.

But if you only have a $200 deductible, you need to file a claim with the company for the $100 they will owe you, and you will have to follow the insurance company's procedures to determine the amount of damages. They don't just write you a check for the $100. It can be hours of paperwork and hassle for that $100.

Chapter Thirty-one
Alternatives

F red went back to working on his future business of founding a
university. He was surprised at how many decisions he would have
to make. Some were big decisions, such as where he would locate
Fred's University. Some were small, such as what brand of chalkboard or
white board he would put in each classroom.

Most of the small decisions—as to chalkboards, chairs, and
curtains—could be put off until a year before opening day. But a lot of
things depended on where he would locate his university. It was a
decision he would have to make sooner rather than later.

Fred did a lot of reading about places in the United States and in
other countries. There were ten factors he wanted to consider.
- ❀ Climate
- ❀ Prices for renting space or for buying existing universities
- ❀ Earthquakes, hurricanes, tornados, floods
- ❀ The number of students and ability to pay
- ❀ The local government regulations
- ❀ Crime rates
- ❀ The local taxes his university would have to pay
- ❀ Competition from other local universities
- ❀ Availability of teachers
- ❀ Small town vs. big city

Initially, Fred started with 170 possible locations. He knew that it
would take years to decide if he were to investigate all ten factors for each
of the 170 locations. (The math: $10 \times 170 = 1{,}700$ research projects)

It seemed to Fred like there were 170 doors that were open to him,
and they all looked good. The weather might be great in one spot, but
there might be too many local government regulations there. In another
spot there might be a need for higher education, but getting teachers might
be more difficult.

Fred didn't want to close any doors.

Story Time

Once upon a time, there was a guy who loved onion rings. That was the only food that he would eat. One day he was really hungry. He sat down for lunch at the dining room table.

There were two plates of hot onion rings. They were each five feet away from him, one on his left and one on his right.

He looked at the left plate. It looked delicious. He looked at the right plate. It looked delicious. If there had only been one plate, he would have eaten it in 20 seconds.

He had too many options.

He couldn't decide.

He starved to death.

the end

Fred had too many options to choose among.* If he waited until he knew everything about all 170 locations, he would be an old man.

One big barrier to super success is a psychological aversion to making decisions that closes off any of our alternatives. It hurts to eliminate any option.

But if you don't close some doors, you end up like the guy with the onion rings.

Fred at 115

Which major in college do you choose? The student who just can't decide winds up with a double (or sometimes a triple) major and takes forever to get through college.

I am a French-lit and chem major.

---

* If there are two options, you choose *between* them. If there are more than two, then you choose *among* them.

You love playing the piano and dream of being a concert pianist. You know that you will have to practice five hours a day to achieve that goal. You also love baseball and dream of becoming a professional baseball player. Another five hours a day. You also have to urge to be a missionary in Kuala Lumpur.*

The marriage ceremony is your announcement to the world that you are closing doors—that you will be true to one (1) other person.

A hundred lifetimes would be much too short to do everything and see everything. Sorry. That's reality.

You gotta close doors, regardless of how painful that will be. If you don't, you will not really succeed in anything.

AND NOW THE ARGUMENT FOR THE OTHER SIDE
DON'T CLOSE TOO MANY DOORS

What does success mean? Does it mean that you will have the most famous pizza restaurant in the world? Or the most money? Or the presidency? Or the best wife/husband?

You can be in the top one or two hundred people in the world in almost any category, given reasonable talent and insanely concentrated work habits.

But in the last hour before your death, you might be thinking about whether you really lived a life. Was it worth it to achieve "the top" and hate your life, have gone through four spouses, not been a good parent to your kids, and not really had many close friends?

You don't need to live an unbalanced life in order to retire in 24 years. You can still be there when your kids are growing up, celebrate your spouse, take some time to putter, and have a hobby that renews you. You can do all of these things and put in 40–60 hours a week toward your career goal—and still get eight hours of sleep each night.

The trick is not to waste time.

---

* Kuala Lumpur is the capital of Malaysia.

It's not wasting time if you have a hobby that clears your mind and enables you to balance work and play.

It's not wasting time if you spend an hour sharing with your loved ones the fears, the hopes, and the dreams that each of you have.

It's not wasting time if you share with God the fears, the hopes, and the dreams that you have.

Each of us, individually, knows when we are wasting time and running away from life—doing the things that just avoid engagement. *What might be wasting time for one person might be central in another's life.*

For example . . .

Learning that $x = \dfrac{-b \pm \sqrt{b^2 - 4ac}}{2a}$ is the solution to $ax^2 + bx + c = 0$

Studying the history of Armenia.

Mastering the new computer-driven sewing machines.

Riding a horse in the park.

Watching quiz shows on TV.

Making silly lists.

Fred knew that he would get nowhere if he retained 170 locations on his list. If he eliminated one of them, that could be eliminating the very best one. But he had to close doors; he had to take the risk.

He plunged. He picked the climate factor. He eliminated places that were too cold. (That crossed off spots in Maine.) He eliminated places with too much rainfall. (That eliminated Quinault, Washington, which has an average annual rainfall of 115.62 inches. That's about an inch of rain every three days on the average.) He eliminated places that had more than thirty 90° days a year. Fred narrowed the list down to 31 places.

Then he crossed off those that had frequent hurricanes, floods, and tornados. He was now down to a manageable seven spots. Two of them were in high crime areas. He was now down to five possible places for the Fred's University.

This was painful work. He liked Quinault for a lot of reasons. He liked Kansas spots, but they were gone with the wind.

Chapter Thirty-two
The Grim Reaper—Taxes

There are many barriers to achieving financial goals. People first starting out on the 24-year road face:

 Lack of startup capital

 Lack of knowledge about the business

 Lack of mentors

 Possibly being too young—being 6 years old is a definite drawback

 Not enough failures, which teach you that you really have to work hard

 Lack of a supportive spouse

 Not having made a tentative choice as to which business

 Not having closed enough doors

On the other hand there are many advantages to the person just starting out. You are more likely to have your health. You are more likely to sense the latest trends and fashions. (Desktop computers ⇒ laptops ⇒ those little things that you hold in your hand*) You are less likely to have a large staff and have invested decades in a dying industry. You are less likely to have to be paying alimony and child support. Your taxes will be relatively low.

----

* This shows you where I, your author, am at in terms of keeping up. I don't even own a cell phone.

When you are into your fourth year (roughly speaking) of your own business and it is starting to pay off, then you will have the chance to delegate more of the day-to-day management to others and get nine hours of sleep a night if you want it.*

Taxes

There are many hindrances to your further business success once you have started to acquire wealth.

Changing technology can put a real crimp in your photographic film manufacturing.

Natural disasters and war can decrease sales.

Union strikes or the death of your top manager can make things difficult.

But the biggest drag on your progress will often be government taxes. There are taxes everywhere—some of them are obvious and others are hidden. There are seven major categories of taxes: 1. Income Taxes, 2. Property Taxes, 3. Consumption Taxes, 4. General Corporation Taxes, 5. Payroll Taxes, 6. Capital Gains Taxes, and 7. Inheritance Taxes.

---

* It is easy to accidentally hire bums who will give you nothing but grief. Learning to fire them quickly is an essential skill to learn.

You can, without too much effort, hire pleasant people who will give you a smile each morning. They will be loyal and they can do simple repetitive tasks and free up hours of your time during the easy startup years. Never promote them to manager level positions.

It's difficult to hire managers, because they should be in the top five percent—smart and adept. Many will have skills that you don't have.

For as long as possible, you should do the hiring and not your managers. It is very difficult for managers to hire top people because those people can be a threat to their own job security. It will be hard enough for you to avoid the temptation of just hiring nice yes-men and yes-women for your business who will make you look smarter but will not contribute as much to making your business prosper.

Every time you turn around, the government (at the federal, state, and local levels) has a hand in your pocket: Accounts Receivable Tax, Alcohol Tax, Building Permit Tax, Capital Gains Tax, Cigarette and Tobacco Tax, Corporate Income Tax, Death Tax, Dog License Tax, Federal Income Tax, Federal Unemployment Tax (FUTA), Fishing License Tax, Food License Tax, Fuel Permit Tax, Fur Clothing Tax, Gasoline Tax, Gift Taxes, Horse Race Admissions Tax, Hotel Room Occupancy Tax, Hunting License Tax, Inheritance Tax, Inventory tax, Local Income Tax, Luxury Taxes, Marriage License Tax, Medicare Tax, Mineral Taxes, Petroleum Taxes, Property Tax, Real Property Transfer Tax, Retail Beer, Wine and Liquor License Taxes, Septic Permit Tax, Social Security Tax, Road Usage Taxes (Truckers), Sales Taxes, Recreational Vehicle Tax, Road Toll Booth Taxes, School Tax, State Income Tax, State Unemployment Tax (SUTA), Tariffs, Telephone Federal Excise Tax, Telephone Federal Universal Service Fee Tax, Telephone Federal, State and Local Surcharge Taxes, Telephone Minimum Usage Surcharge Tax, Telephone Usage Charge Tax, Toll Bridge Taxes, Toll Tunnel Taxes, Trailer Registration Tax, Utility Taxes, Vehicle License Registration Tax, Vehicle Sales Tax, Watercraft Registration Tax, Well Permit Tax, Wind Energy Production Tax, Workers Compensation Tax.

One of the less hidden taxes is the sales tax. In parts of Alabama, Louisiana, and Oklahoma the sales tax is 11%.

Imagine standing at the checkout of one of those big stores like Wal-Mart, Costco, or Sam's Club and getting 11% of every purchase? Could you run a state and local government on that much money? I think I could. And I'd abolish all the other state and local taxes.

Imagine you were living in one of those 11% sales tax areas and you needed to spend $10,000 for equipment and supplies for your business. You could get 11% more ($1,100) if you were living in parts of Oregon where there is no sales tax. You'd be 11% richer.

THE INCOME TAX

A 1913 amendment to the Constitution created the Federal income tax. Before that time, the direct taxes of the Federal government had to be proportional to the population of each state. (Article I, Section 2) Everyone was treated alike.

After 1913 the rules changed. The more productive you were, the more you had to pay. Worse than that: If you were twice as productive, you might have to pay three times as much tax.

What does this do to a person's desire to work? Suppose you are in California and earning as much as Fred might be earning in his fourth year of Fred's University. It's November and you are in the top tax rate brackets. The Federal income tax will take 40% of what you earn today. The State of California will take over 10% of what you earn today.

You work eight hours and four of them are taken from you. Why not take the day off? Making money gives you **HaPPiNeSS PoiNtS**, but leisure time activities also give you happiness points. Under heavy taxation, the productivity of a nation declines.

A slave is defined as someone who does not receive the fruits of his/her work. If the master takes half of what you have produced, you aren't free. Life, liberty, and property are all tied together.

THE REAL WEALTH OF A SOCIETY IS CREATED.

Wealth is not a fixed amount that is merely transferred among its citizens.

Take someone and drop him onto some uninhabited land. He has nothing. Zero wealth.

He finds a sharp rock and makes an ax. (The ax is something that was not there before. It is the start of wealth.)

He cuts trees and makes a log cabin. (Real estate!)

Fred's Cabin

He makes a bow and arrow and a fishing pole. He hunts and fishes. What he doesn't eat and keeps is more wealth. (Deer jerky?)

He mines the earth for iron.

And after several more years (centuries?) he is manufacturing computers and coffee machines.

This is no fantasy story. This is **THE STORY OF CIVILIZATION**. Wealth is created by those who work. We are not fighting over a fixed piece of pie (unless no one is working).

Before the passage of the income tax amendment in 1913, the bulk of the federal government revenue was from taxes on imports, called customs duties. And about a third of the revenue came from taxes on alcohol.

After the income tax amendment, Congress and the president were swimming in revenues from the income tax.

A Short History of Alcohol Prohibition

For many years before 1913, there was a strong movement to prohibit alcohol. Ever since the days of Noah, alcohol abuse has plagued our world.* There was a strong push by the public for Congress to outlaw alcohol. Did they do it? Of course not. Liquor taxes were a third of Congress's income. Getting money was more important than what the people wanted.

After the income tax receipts were flowing in, liquor taxes weren't that important. Congress could now bow to public pressure. The 18th Amendment–Prohibition–was passed.

The rest of the story happened in the early years of the Depression. People weren't making as much money and didn't have to pay as much in income taxes. Public opinion had not much changed. Most still didn't want alcohol to be legal. But the federal government needed money. In 1934 the 21st Amendment repealed alcohol prohibition and new tax moneys flowed in.

Nowadays, will we see the repeal of some of the drug laws (marijuana, for example) so that those drugs can be taxed?

---

* The National Institute on Alcohol Abuse and Alcoholism reported that for college students (age 18–24) in 2002, there were 1,400 deaths and 70,000 sexual assaults caused by alcohol.

How you make your money can affect your tax rates. For the federal income taxes and the state income taxes, wages are often taxed at the highest rates. If you buy something (such as stocks) and sell it at a profit in a short period of time (say, less than a year), you have short-term capital gains—often taxed at a lower rate than wages.

Buy and sell for a profit in a longer period of time and you have long-term capital gains—taxed at a lower rate than short-term gains.

The federal laws for taxes change almost every year. Sometimes there are small changes; sometimes large changes. That makes it difficult to plan ahead. Large businesses are sometimes required to submit tax returns that are thousands of pages long. Even before they pay a dollar in taxes, significant amounts are spent figuring out how much they owe.

Chapter Thirty-three
Democracy on a Desert Island

With one day left before classes began, Fred was taking his last opportunity (before Saturday) to get in a full day's work on his future business of founding a university. He had narrowed his search for the site of Fred's University down to five places. He decided to head off to the KITTENS University library to see if there were any books on those five places.

He said goodbye to Kingie (who was still painting), headed down the hallway, down the two flights of stairs, and jogged across the campus. Within minutes, he had a list of the call numbers of the books he wanted to look at and was gathering them off the library shelves. One of the librarians walked with him. Fred could pick the books he wanted off the lower shelves, and she would reach the books off the top shelves.

They carried the books to a library table. Fred thanked the librarian and sat down to read.

He read about the state and local regulations in those five cities. He read about what were the popular majors in those cities. It wasn't surprising when he learned that oceanography wasn't very popular as a major in Colorado.

Then Fred noticed a book he wasn't expecting: *The Diary of Fredrika*. The librarian had apparently pulled the wrong book off the shelf. Fred liked the picture of her on the front cover. He opened the book and read of her adventures.

March 20th. On board the cruise ship Lollipop. Having a wonderful time. Wonderful weather in the South Seas.

March 21st. Pirates attack. We offer them doughnuts if they will just leave us alone. They sink the ship. Ten of us escape and swim to deserted island.

March 22nd. We meet to discuss our future. One guy says that we don't have to worry, that we would be rescued soon. Another guy asks how he knows that. The first guy said that he left a trail of doughnuts floating in the water on the way toward out island. The second guy said that he couldn't see any doughnuts in the water. All he could see was a very fat fish.

Fred liked the way Fredrika drew pictures.

my drawing

March 23rd. We meet again. Everyone agrees that we will probably be here a long time. We have to figure out the rules for our "little nation." That's what we call it.

One guy suggested that we operate by consensus. The only rules would be the ones that we all agree on. Another guy said that was stupid and "If we could all agree on a rule, then why make that a rule at all." We couldn't all agree on the consensus approach.

One guy who was 6'6" tall and must have had 300 pounds of pure muscle announced that our little nation would be ruled by him. He would be king and make the rules. The rest of us jumped on him and beat the tar out of him.

One guy suggested, "Let's do it the traditional Judeo-Christian American way: a democracy."

Fred almost broke out laughing when he read this. Democracy is not big in the Old Testament. They had a lot of kings back then. Democracy in the New Testament? Did Jesus ever call for a vote? Democracy in America? That word is not mentioned in the Declaration of Independence or in the Constitution. The United States of America is a **republic**, not a **democracy**.*

Another guy said, "Let's put it to a vote. All in favor of a democracy say yea."

I shouted, "Wait a minute! There's something nutty going on here. You are assuming you have a democracy already—where the vote of the majority becomes the law for all."

I was outvoted.

From now on what 6 of the 10 of us agree on, will be the law for all of us.

April 3rd. Most of the guys just sit around eating bananas and playing touch football all day. Pat and I are the only ones who are working

---

* Look up *republic* and *democracy* in any good dictionary.

hard. Pat has been making fishing nets. I've been making hula skirts. I know that it won't be many more months before our clothes start to wear out and rip—given the harsh sand and sun.

April 15th. A meeting is called. By a vote of 8 to 2, the Share Our Wealth law is passed. Everyone has to share what they've produced with everyone else. They claim this is fair—everyone is treated alike. They said that they needed to close the big gap between the wealthy and the poor—between us two and those eight.

Ha! Only Pat and I have been producing anything. What we own is now owned by the group.

Fred shut the book. He didn't want to read any more of this sad story.

*The big danger in a democracy
is what it does to the minorities.*

Hitler was democratically elected. The Jews were a minority.

Wait a minute! I, your reader, am confused! Where do you, the author, stand? You aren't arguing for a king or a dictator. You seem to be saying that democracy is bad. What's left? Are you an anarchist who believes in no laws at all?

I'm glad you asked. I also vote No on anarchy.

Okay. What's left?

Let's look at Fredrika and the other nine who live on the same island as she does. I am in favor of laws against murder, purse snatching,* counterfeiting checks, and all the other things that C.C. Coalback does. Each of those on the island should be allowed to live in peace as long as they don't do bad things to others. *The only laws that should be made are those that protect people from the aggression of others.* It's that simple.

The government should not be the aggressor against its citizens. If I'm not hurting my neighbors, I shouldn't have government officials knocking on my door.

---

* Years ago my mother was standing at a bus stop in San Francisco when a man grabbed her purse and ran to a waiting car. I wish I had been there when that happened.

Today, the federal government has military bases in more than 120 foreign countries.

Today, part of the income tax money that I'm forced to pay goes toward subsidies to tobacco farmers.

Today, Uncle Sam takes my money and gives it to foreign countries ("foreign aid").

Hey. You haven't answered my question. What's it going to be: kings or democracy?

What I'm trying to say is that's the wrong question. I really don't care if a king makes the laws or if Congress makes the laws. What I care about is that the king or the Congress has limited powers—only making laws to protect the individual citizens.

And how in blazes are you going to make sure they don't make laws that overstep those limited powers?

Easy. You have a law that the king or the Congress must obey—a law higher than the lawmakers.

That's impossible!

You are mistaken. In this country it is called the Constitution. Back in Chapter 18, I talked about how the Constitution limits the power of the federal government. The Bill of Rights (the first ten amendments) further limits government so that it does not trespass on our liberty.*
Amendment 1: "*Congress shall make no law respecting an establishment or religion . . . speech . . . the press . . . peaceable assembly . . . .*"
Amendment 2: ". . . *right of the people to keep and bear arms.*"
None of the Bills of Rights adds power to the federal government.

Almost 70% of individual income tax filers today use Form 1040EZ with its 12 little lines to fill out. And they vote to take from the minority top producers just as it happened on Fredrika's island. In 2010 the top 1% paid almost as much in taxes as the bottom 95%. ($354.8 billion vs. $388.4 billion). And half of that bottom group paid no taxes at all. And since 2010 it's gotten even more punishing for those who produce.

---

* Liberty is a very special word. It doesn't just mean freedom. It means freedom from a government that makes unjust laws—laws that go beyond protecting the people. Every U.S. coin has the word LIBERTY on it.

Chapter Thirty-four
Sunk Costs

Founding a university was Fred's goal. He read the books in the library to find out, among other things, how much it would cost him in terms of time, money, effort, and pain to achieve that goal. Once he learned that cost, he had to decide whether he was willing to pay that cost. Every goal in life needs to be looked at from those two angles: what's the cost and am I willing to pay it. This is called the **future**.

The **past** is different. The cost does not matter and there is no decision as to whether you'll pay it. Costs in the past are called **sunk costs**. They have been paid, and there are no refunds.

People who can't tell the future from the past often make terrible choices. They lose a lot of happiness points—financial and otherwise.

For example, you buy a stock at $100 and it goes down to $70. The $100 is a sunk cost. It's been paid. That's in the past. When you bought it at $100, that was the best alternative *at that time*. But that time is not now. You are living in (drum roll please . . .) the **present**. You have to make a decision now. Many people are tempted to look back to that $100. They think I'll wait till the stock goes back to $100 and then sell it. That is the wrong approach. What they are really trying to do is not suffer a failure. They don't want to look bad.*

Looking back is silly

Instead, live in the present. You own a stock that is currently priced at $70. Your goal (future) is to make money. It isn't to look good. The question to look at is What do I think this stock is worth right now? You need to guess what its price will be. The $100 is irrelevant. If you think the price will rise, then you buy more.

The key point for any investment you own is to pretend you don't own it and ask yourself whether you would buy it today. If you wouldn't buy it today, sell it!

Selling is psychologically much harder than buying.

---

* They never read Chapter 26 ("Failure") of this book.

You spend years and a hundred thousand dollars to become a dentist and set up your business. For a year you have been drilling, filling, and billing. You realize that today there is little joy in dentistry for you.

The years of schooling are sunk costs. The huge amount of money you have spent are sunk costs.

What really matters is the decision you have to make right now. Pretend you don't own it (the dentistry practice) and ask yourself whether you would "buy" it today.

You have a choice tomorrow morning when you are still in bed. Choice #1: You could head to your dental office and effortlessly continue fixing teeth. You don't count the sunk costs. You might be bored, but you will make a very decent income. You can afford almost any vacation that appeals to you.
Choice #2: You can stay in bed. Close the dental office. Your mother will not approve of this choice.
Choice #3: You can launch a new career as a carpenter (or whatever).

It's important to note that big decisions (change of career, marriage, joining the army for six years) should not be made on the spur of the moment.

Fred chose to charge ahead in his quest to found a university. He finished reading the stack of books and carried them to the librarian so that she could reshelve them.

He was aware that six years down this road he might encounter an insurmountable barrier. The government might, for example, prohibit the founding of new universities or make the licensing costs so high that new universities couldn't be created. (The existing universities would love this kind of legislation.)

Or he might discover that with all the free education on the Internet, the need wasn't there for another teaching institution. Instead, he might found Fred's Testing and Certification Center, which would specialize in evaluating what students have learned (from any source) and granting Fred Certificates that employers could trust.

Or it just might be true that someday there will be a Fred's University.

Index

*To learn more about Fred
and other books about him
visit*

FredGauss.com